WHEN LEADERS MATTER

How **Civility, Integrity,** and the Leaders We Need **Are Possible**

Dr. Joel W. Harder

ISBN: 978-1-943361-65-6

E-Book ISBN: 978-1-943361-66-3

Library of Congress Control Number: 2019919260

Printed in the United States of America.

Dedication

For Donelle, Philece, and Farrow.

Contents

Foreword

★ ★ ★ ★ ★

I have always believed in the power of listening to others. Everyone has a voice and a story, and every voice is important. Over and over again, I discover there is always something I can learn from listening to the people around me. It is when more people are willing to share their different perspectives and experiences that I become a better leader. That was true in my business, with my family and friends, and now as Governor of Oklahoma. I have always been convinced Oklahoma can be a top ten state. We have the best people, great opportunity, and all the resources we need to get there, but it will take all of us to do it.

The first time I met Chaplain Joel Harder was at lunch in Norman, Oklahoma. I asked him about his work at the capitol and he asked me about my vision for the state of Oklahoma. Then, he asked if he could pray for me and I learned a few things pretty quickly about him. Joel has a deep faith that God is working in our lives and has a purpose for each of us. He believes, like I do, that everyone's voice is important. He sets politics aside and understands the personal responsibility leaders carry as we do our work to the best of our ability.

I've also seen Joel put his beliefs into practice with leaders across the Oklahoma State Capitol as he works with my colleagues in the Oklahoma Senate, House of Representatives, as well as members of my administration and staff. He consistently interacts with Oklahoma's elected leaders in a way that is always encouraging, prayerful, and a welcome help to our work at the Capitol.

Here are my three main takeaways from this book:

WHEN LEADERS MATTER
★ ★ ★ ★ ★

1. *Praying for leaders, their work, and their families is at the heart of this book.* I recognize the difference prayer makes in my own life and knowing there are people praying for me and my family is among the greatest encouragements I get as governor. As you read *When Leaders Matter,* I trust you will be inspired as I am to pray for leaders across our state and nation.

2. *All of us have the ability to engage leaders and make a positive difference.* The book presents a practical way for anyone to approach elected leaders that breaks through the conflict and incivility we often see in politics.

3. *Integrity is one of the most important things we need in leaders today.* The book looks at nine qualities of integrity. They are characteristics that I admire in the leaders around me and ones I aspire to have in my own life especially serving as the Governor of Oklahoma. Integrity is not only important in leaders but in all of us, and we can help the next generation of leaders develop the very qualities that will serve us best in the future.

I believe, as Joel does, that the civility, integrity, and leaders we need in Oklahoma and across the nation are possible. This book reminded me that my voice is important and I can be part of changing the tone in politics today. This book challenged me to look for ways to sharpen my leadership abilities and helped me know how to better pray for leaders.

Signed,
Kevin Stitt
Governor of Oklahoma
December 13, 2019

Introduction

★ ★ ★ ★ ★

Ask More *of* Leaders by Asking More *for* Leaders

Our culture is struggling. Particularly in politics today, people are bitterly divided, angry, hostile, and fearful. Is this simply the way American political discourse is going to be? How are civility, integrity, and the leaders we need possible in the years ahead?

It starts with you because we are all responsible for our culture. It has been said that leaders are downstream of culture. If that is true, then restoring civility and producing leaders who will model integrity is only possible if that is what each of us expect and demand. But how much can one person accomplish? How much power or influence do you really have?

The answer is, probably more than you think. Years of working with elected leaders and serving as a chaplain to the Oklahoma House of Representatives has shown me it is possible to break cycles of incivility. I have seen the opportunity one person can have to engage leaders in state and local government in a way that breaks through partisan gridlock.

We begin with leaders because leaders matter. It has also been said that leaders set the tone. That is true in any organization, as well as in society at large and in politics. Leaders matter because they are in unique positions of authority and influence. As a chaplain in the Oklahoma legislature, I meet people from all across the state, in both political parties, and from all walks of life who come to the Oklahoma State Capitol to meet with their elected leaders. They come to make their voices heard and express concerns, typically over a particular policy debate raging in the legislature. Others come to the Capitol because of a specific need or challenge in their community. In almost every instance, they come to ask something of their leaders because leaders have the power to solve *real* problems.

The state of public discourse in American politics today is a *real* problem. Even if leaders are downstream of this culture, they are the people in positions of authority and influence who can inspire us to desire better. I have seen it happen. I've watched the political culture completely transform when leaders were willing to seek better. I've witnessed state and local leaders work together to frustrate tired political narratives by bringing diverse people to the table to find common ground. Those are the leaders and conversations that move us forward and the reason I believe the civility, integrity, and leaders we need are possible.

Now is the time when we should ask more of the people serving in public office; this is why the title of this book is *When Leaders Matter*. They matter right now. This is the time for people who will lead us out from the incivility, hostility, and vitriol permeating our public discourse to step forward. Of course, we cannot expect such leaders to emerge on their own. Respect and integrity are qualities we can develop in future leaders. But these are also the qualities we can ask of those already in leadership—if we are willing to.

How we choose to engage leaders is the subject of this book. In the pages that follow, I will share a specific approach to engaging leaders in a way that breaks through the problem of incivility, particularly in our political discourse. Years of working with political leaders, both in Washington and in the Oklahoma State Capitol, have shown me time and again that when everyday people from all walks of life approach elected leaders with three simple steps, they discover their own power and ability to help solve problems and break through the incivility.

Step One: *Believe* Leaders Matter

Step Two: Ask More *for* Leaders

Step Three: Ask More *of* Leaders

The first step of this process—*believe* leaders matter—recognizes the unique role of leaders to exercise real authority in society while emphasizing the importance of remembering that leaders are people. Leaders quickly become caricatures of themselves based on our prejudices and personal opinions of the politics, party, policies, or principles they seem to represent. While power and authority exist and are necessary components in the world, there is a difference between the positions of leadership where power is found and the individuals who are in those positions. The position is not the same as the person.

Step two is asking more *for* leaders. Now that you are able to better distinguish between the leadership position and the person in that place of authority, you can better approach them and interact with respect and sincerity. Before you ever ask anything *of* a leader, first ask more *for* leaders—specifically, by expressing gratitude and sincerely desiring the best for their lives, families, and homes.

Now comes step three, asking more *of* leaders. Maybe what you would like to ask of a leader pertains to a particular problem or challenge in your life or community. There are actions leaders can take and policies they can champion that will make a difference. It is right and appropriate to have those discussions with leaders, and we expect leaders to faithfully fulfill the functions of their authority. Before this, consider one more implication to thinking of leaders first of all as people. What we need most of a leader is that they are a person of integrity. This is the more we should ask *of* leaders and what we can ask *for* them.

Engaging leaders through this three-step approach produces the type of respectful political discourse we need and breaks through the incivility dividing homes, communities, states, and our nation. Practicing this approach to engaging leaders helps each of us discover the power within us to positively shape the culture of our politics. Finally, the kind of person who engages leaders and politics in this way is becoming the very kind of leader we need in the future.

What This Book Is Not

This is not a book *on* leadership insomuch that it presents particular leadership practices, models, or principles. In other words, this is not a "how to" book on leadership. While Chapters 1 and 2 draw upon well-established theories and research to argue the function of leadership in society and defend the premise that leaders matter, they are not a critical discussion on the merits of any particular leadership philosophy.

Saying this is not a book on leadership also means it is not a study of the lives or examples of great leaders in the past or present. That said, I derived the three-step process for engaging leaders from the lives and practices of actual leaders in history. Chapters 3, 4, and 5 will analyze the methods, strategies, life, and writings of the Apostle Paul, one of Christianity's most significant early leaders. Additionally, step three of this book is presented in Chapters 9-13, which offer a profile of the leaders we need by exploring nine qualities that mark a person of integrity.

Second, this is not a book *about* Jesus or the Bible, and my approach to engaging leaders is not only for Christians or those who share my views of the Bible or the function of prayer. However, this approach to engaging leaders could not exist without Jesus and the Bible. I unashamedly base the approach outlined in this book on principles found in Scripture, and that is why whole chapters will examine certain biblical passages. Saying this is not a book about

Jesus or the Bible means it is not necessary to first adopt certain beliefs about God, Jesus Christ, the Bible, or prayer in order to engage leaders through this method. This approach can be beneficial whatever you may believe about the Bible or prayer. What I am asking is this: consider how the Bible remains a relevant source of wisdom and can effectively guide us out of the cultural incivility permeating our politics.

Finally, this book is not the ramblings of a *naïve* optimist. I present this approach to engaging leaders with sincere hope, believing we can break through the incivility gripping American political discourse. But I realize hope-filled optimism about the current political moment can seem idealistic or impractical. I am aware how the political process delivers both progress and frustration. The same leaders who inspire us also let us down and the promises of public policy stand next to unintended consequences. Just as leaders matter—as the title of this book suggests—so do political campaigns. While the ideas championed by candidates running for office are an important part of shaping the political conversation, the ultimate goal of a campaign is to win the election. Shaping a positive leadership culture in politics and breaking through the incivility in political discourse requires us to ask more of leaders without ignoring political realities.

Politics can be a nasty business, and we need leaders who maintain integrity and model servant leadership as they navigate the often-muddied waters of the political process. Such leaders are possible. You probably agree, or you would not be reading this book. Such leaders already exist and need our encouragement and prayers to persevere in their legislative task and work for the good of all people in their communities, states, and our nation.

Brief Thoughts about the Bible

While you do not need to share my views of the Bible, it is appropriate to briefly explain my views as much of this book draws upon various passages and principles from Scripture. Beliefs about the nature of the Bible obviously differ among people of faiths other than Christianity, as well as those who hold to no faith. Within Christianity itself, opinions of the Bible vary widely. Donald McKim discusses twelve different interpretations of the nature of Scripture in his book *What Christians Believe About the Bible*. Roger Olsen comments on the ranging interpretations of Scripture in *The Mosaic of Christian Belief*, writing, "On the surface there may seem little or no unity among Christians with regard to the Bible."[1] Describing these differing interpretations, Olsen goes on to say, "Some Christians view the Bible as that manuscript from heaven" while others regard the Bible as "nothing more than a (or the) Christian classic."[2]

In total transparency, I have a *high view* of the nature and function of Scripture and agree with John Wesley, the founder of the Methodist Movement, who believed all Scripture is inspired of God: "[The] Spirit of God not only once inspired those who wrote it, but continually inspires, supernaturally assists, those that read it with earnest prayer."[3] Believing Scripture is inspired by God, the Bible informs how I understand the events of the world around me, and I find, "The fear of the Lord *(really) is* the beginning of wisdom, and the knowledge of the Holy One is understanding."[4]

For those who share this belief, the Bible guides us in how we relate to others and immerse ourselves in the culture in which we live. This is what is meant by developing a *biblical worldview,* where the Bible becomes the lens through which a person understands themselves and everything in the world around them. Holding a biblical worldview means the Bible shapes my understanding of how the world began (cosmology), the value of human beings as well as their behavior (anthropology), the nature of God and His interaction with the world (theology), and where the course of human events lead (eschatology).

INTRODUCTION
★ ★ ★ ★ ★

Claiming a biblical worldview does not deny other sources of wisdom and knowledge that provide insight into understanding the world, such as the branches of science, philosophy, culture, and art. But the Bible has special authority above other sources of knowledge "because it is penetrated and filled with the Holy Spirit."[5] The presence of God's own Spirit within the text has two important implications. First, the Bible uniquely reveals the person and work of God. Second, it invites everyone who desires to encounter God to experience Him:

> [The Bible] is the vehicle of God's grace and is uniquely used by God to bring people into a transforming encounter with God that informs and changes them . . . Because God chose [the Bible] to be this unique instrument and witness, it has always been since its inception a unique authority to which Christians turn for guidance.[6]

Derived from the Latin, *scriptura*, "*Scripture* is the historic Judeo-Christian name for the specific literature that the church receives as divine instruction, that is, as God's own witness to himself . . . concerning his work, will, and ways."[7] In other words, the Bible is a collection of many unique books which collectively tell one story of God's nature and power as He redeems and prepares a people with whom to dwell in holiness, love, and fellowship.[8]

In telling this story, I find the Bible to be a thoroughly cogent, internally consistent, and enduring source of wisdom that transcends time and culture. The Bible tells us where we came from and where we are going and explains everything that is wrong in the world and precisely how everything is being set right. The good news found in the Bible is how the failures and flaws that every person has are resolved as they come to know the God who created them through Jesus. The same process of personal redemption applies to every person on earth, in every generation, and in every possible place or cultural circumstance—no matter the particular religious traditions or legal structures. There is no other book like it. The essential teachings of the Bible apply equally to a suburb of Oklahoma City, a slum in India, and a prison cell in Soviet Russia.

As biblical principles become the foundation for truth to the reader, the Bible also becomes a trusted guide into every subject area of life. But we must understand what is not in the Bible. Like every other book, there is limited information conveyed in the Bible. The response is often to criticize Scripture for not speaking exhaustively on subjects that matter to us at particular times and for various reasons. The flaw in this critique is that it asks the Bible to tell *my* story. It doesn't. The Bible tells us *God's* story, which is better by far. The miracle of understanding God's story, as it is revealed in the Bible, is how people from every generation and nation around the world become part of this story and find eternal purpose for their lives. The Bible invites us into God's family and teaches us to recognize God's voice. Roger Olsen writes the following explanation:

> Apart from the Holy Spirit the Bible would be to the sinner a dead book. But in the "hands" of the Spirit of God the Bible has always again and again become the unique instrument that shapes the identity of God's people and transforms their lives.[9]

Finally, be careful to consider all the Bible has to say on a subject when looking there for guidance. This is called finding the consensus of Scripture. The biblical authors themselves speak of the value and necessity of considering all the Bible has to say. Before departing Ephesus, Paul reminded the people that he declared the "whole plan of God" to them, and he issued a warning:

> Men will rise up even from your own number and distort the truth to lure the disciples into following them . . . And now I commit you to God and to the word of his grace, which is

able to build you up and to give you an inheritance among all who are sanctified.[10]

Seeking the whole counsel of God keeps us from confusion about God's character and from believing distortions of the truth; it shows us how to know God through the life of Jesus Christ. Seeking the whole counsel of God also informs every aspect of life. Writing to Timothy, the Apostle Paul clearly states his view of Scripture: "All Scripture is inspired by God and is profitable for teaching, for rebuking, for correcting, for training in righteousness, so that the man of God may be complete, equipped for every good work."[11] I agree with Paul's statement and summarize my thoughts on the Bible in this way:

It is the height of arrogance to impose our beliefs upon Scripture.

It is the depth of depravity to manipulate Scripture.

It is the mark of humility to seek the wisdom found in Scripture.

It is the fullness of humanity to follow the pattern of Scripture.

Where This Is All Headed

I am hopeful for the future of America's political culture and public discourse and believe in the resiliency of American democracy. I further believe there are eternal purposes for the events of our lives and in the world. My hope and belief are established in two passages of Scripture, the first from the ancient wisdom found in Proverbs 4:18: "The path of the righteous is like the light of dawn, shining brighter and brighter until midday." The second passage is Revelation 21:5: "Then the One seated on the throne said, 'Look, I am making everything new.'" From these two verses, I conclude that we need never fear a future where God is seated on the throne.

I am also committed to the great promise of the gospel that through the Holy Spirit, God is transforming people through the renewing of their minds until they attain the *fully human life* they were intended to live.[12] For the Christian, the fully human life is neither blindly aspirational nor vaguely defined. Michael Wilkins explains that a person can "live a fully human life in this world in union with Jesus Christ and growing in conformity to his image."[13] The fully human life is rooted in the concrete example of a real person who lived, died, and was raised back to life. Furthermore, attaining the fully human life is the promised destiny for anyone who believes the gospel recorded in the writings of the New Testament. In his letter to the churches in Rome, Paul teaches that every day of our life is drawing us nearer to the time when we will be perfectly conformed to image of Jesus Christ. He writes, "We know that all things work together for the good of those who love God, who are called according to his purpose. For those he foreknew he also predestined to be conformed to the image of his Son."[14]

None of us have arrived. The transformation of our hearts, minds, and bodies is a process that takes a lifetime. There are good days when we can see there is a difference, and there are bad days when we fail to think as we should and act in ways we regret. The Bible reassures us that on both the good days and the bad we can be sure "that he who started a good work in you will carry it on completion until the day of Christ Jesus."[15]

Whether this is a good day or bad, each of us have a place in this world where we live, work, and grow. Wherever that is, those who are in this transformation process have a responsibility to the people and place in which they live. You may love your job or go to work each day thinking of how to move on to something else. In either case, we can put our hands to work to the very best of our ability and positively influence the people and places where we live and work until the day comes that we reach the end of the transformation process. At the end of each day, you can be a little better than you were and always one day closer to living the fully human life that God intends for you. Along the way, the world around you can also be a little better because you were in it.

This is what Jesus meant when He called His disciples salt and light in the world. Calling His disciples light, Jesus' metaphor is simple enough to understand. Light exposes the darkness and draws people close to its warmth. Calling us salt, Jesus intends us to have a very real effect on the world around us. Salt draws out what is impure and preserves what is good. John Stott once preached, "Salt and light are not just a bit different from their environment. They are to have a powerful influence on their environment."[16] Mike Metzger of the Clapham Institute describes the influence being salt and light has, stating it demands two things:

> Being salt and light demands two things. We practice purity in the midst of a fallen world and yet we live in proximity to this fallen world. If you don't hold up both truths in tension, you invariably become useless and separated from the world God loves.[17]

I live my life by this philosophy, and some days are better than others. With this view of the world, I want to do all that I can to have the greatest influence possible. That is why I work with leaders and, for the last few years, with elected leaders in the Oklahoma State Capitol. I am at the Capitol because wherever there is a concentration of power and influence, the trials and temptations to abuse or misuse that power will inevitably be fierce. Leaders who maintain integrity and model civility in the political arena are possible when we choose to encourage rather than denigrate. Their character and integrity is tested and refined when they are about the people's work at the Capitol just as much as when they are at home with family, talking to constituents, and in their respective faith communities.

Finally, I work with political leaders while believing civility, integrity, and the leaders we need are possible. Take one look at the political climate, marked by incivility, hostility, and vitriol, and see that we are having more bad days than good. This doesn't have to continue. We can shape a positive leadership culture where public policy is made. I have seen this happen through an intentional approach to engaging leaders that helps them to be better, and I invite you to join me. Ask more *of* leaders, believing that we can break through the culture of incivility plaguing our politics. Ask more *for* leaders because when our leaders are better, we all are better.

This approach:

- Is simple; but let us never be so arrogant to think simple things are not significant.

- Is kind; but let us never be so cynical to think kindness is not contagious.

- Is respectful; but let us never be so resentful to think respecting others does not demand respect.

- Takes time; but let us never be so impatient to think what takes time is not timeless.

Believe Leaders Matter

The greatest leader is not necessarily the one who does the greatest things. He is the one that gets the people to do the greatest things.

—President Ronald Reagan[1]

What is needed now, more than ever, is leadership that steers us away from fear and fosters greater confidence in the inherent goodness and ingenuity of humanity.

—President Jimmy Carter[2]

Knowing their thoughts, he told them: "Every kingdom divided against itself is headed for destruction, and no city or house divided against itself will stand."

—Matthew 12:25

Chapter 1

★ ★ ★ ★ ★

When Shaping the Leadership Culture

Culture makes people understand each other better.
And if they understand each other better in their soul, it is easier
to overcome the economic and political barriers. But first they
have to understand that their neighbor is, in the end, just like
them, with the same problems, the same questions.

—Paulo Coelho[1]

Being Present Is Important

It was late. The enormous stained-glass windows, which span the width of the ceiling, were dark. Their intricate designs and the array of glowing colors that typically warms the ornate chamber were nearly indistinguishable. They looked strange and dull without the light shining behind them. The room felt empty but was not. Nearly all of the 101 chairs were occupied by the one person assigned to each seat. Private conversations created a low hum of noise that seemed to perfectly support the one voice speaking above the rest. The man's voice was calm and methodical. One by one, he addressed the numerous questions and concerns raised by the others. The talking continued, and the night droned further on.

Getting a chair in this room is no small task. It takes months of preparation, countless meetings, public appearances, knocking on doors, and giving speeches. This is the Oklahoma House of Representatives and getting a seat in this room ultimately comes down to a majority of votes cast in each legislative district across the state.

These elected leaders had a difficult task before them. It was well past ten o'clock at night on a cloudy day in May of 2017, and the state was facing a significant budget deficit for the third consecutive year. The legislature hoped to address and resolve the budget shortfall through a complex and long-negotiated bill. Members of the House were clearly concerned by the details of this plan. The bill in question raised new revenue in the state in a plan that grew more contentious with every passing minute. Opinions of each member of the Oklahoma House of Representatives on the bill varied and would eventually come down to a vote later that night. Two important questions remained unanswered: Would the bill pass? How close would they get to the midnight deadline?

Hours earlier, I was sitting at home having dinner with my wife and two young daughters when my phone started to buzz. Representatives were sending text messages and asking for prayer. They were already a few hours into the question and answer period, which would inevitably lead to a lengthy debate where legislators would deliver impassioned speeches supporting or opposing the legislation. I started typing responses, commending each for their patience and letting them know that I was praying for them. I knew tensions were high, so as my wife put our youngest to bed, I grabbed a jacket and Bible and then slipped out the door to head back to the Capitol. Being present is important.

Sitting in the empty gallery above the floor of the House Chamber and under that darkened stained-glass ceiling, I read Psalms and prayed. Representatives joined me upstairs to visit quietly while debate continued on the floor below. The measure narrowly passed the House of Representatives but failed to receive the sufficient number of votes needed to raise revenue as stipulated by the state constitution. After months of negotiation and hours of questions and debate on the floor of the House, this bill would not be the solution to the nearly one-billion-dollar deficit. Tired as the representatives were, the work that the people of Oklahoma sent them to the Capitol to do was far from over.

I stood in the lobby of the House Chamber while members slowly began streaming off the floor to head out for the night. Most were discouraged; some were deeply frustrated. Others gathered in small huddles to begin talking about potential contingencies, alternatives, and next steps. Still other members were just ready to get out of the building for the first time since arriving in the early hours of that morning. All of them were exhausted.

I prayed that night and asked God to use me and, if possible, to rally their spirits. I voiced a simple prayer: "God, some voted yes, and others voted no. They did what they believed was right. It's late, and they are tired, but there will be more to do tomorrow. Use me to encourage them, if I can." After that simple prayer, I shook hands and gave a few pats on the back while smiling to each one and thanking them for their service.

Being present for the events of that night are a regular part of my work as a chaplain in the Oklahoma State Capitol. This is the job. Working as a chaplain in the legislature requires me to walk the halls, attend press conferences and committee hearings, host luncheons, and teach early morning Bible studies. Over time, I have come to know members of both the Oklahoma House of Representatives and Senate from both political parties and on all sides of policy issues. I am honored to count them as friends.

Despite their many differences, our elected leaders share a deep conviction to do what they believe is right to serve the constituents in their districts and all of Oklahoma. I also know that elected leaders

serving in office face enormous pressure. The weeks when the legislature is in session move at a blistering speed. Daily schedules
overflow with appointments and responding to constituent needs.

The responsibility to enact good public policy requires hours
of research and back-to-back meetings with policy experts on all
sides of particular issues. Those same policy experts each represent
various groups and individuals with diverse, often competing interests and positions on wide range of issues. Lawmakers navigate
this fast-paced environment knowing the policies they develop
will ultimately impact the people in most, if not every, community
across the state. The stakes are high, and their days can be stress-
ful. But working in the policy-making arena is also exhilarating and
fulfilling. The work they accomplish affects many.

A chaplain to the state legislature is unique in the political setting
where public policy is decided. A chaplain provides an encouraging presence in what can, at times, be a discouraging place. To do
this effectively requires me to be non-political, non-partisan, and
non-lobbying. I set the labels of leadership position and political
party aside to focus on elected leaders as *people*.

When asked what a typical workday looks like, I respond, "I'm
a fulltime presence in the state Capitol and probably look to most
people like one of the lobbyists. But when an elected leader sees
me, they know I don't want anything *from* them. Instead, I want
something *for* them. I want them to be encouraged. I want them to
know someone is thankful for their work, service, and leadership. I
want them to know someone is praying for them."

This approach allows me to be an effective chaplain, but I
discovered something more. When it comes to leaders, focusing on
the *person* more than their *position*, through an attitude of thankfulness and sincerely desiring the best for them, makes a real difference. Then, the typical and tired political narratives that often stall
constructive policy debate begin to fall apart. I discovered it is

possible to shape a positive leadership culture where public policy is made. Shaping a positive leadership culture means our elected leaders are able to think, work, and lead better. Isn't that what we really want? We need elected leaders constructively solving *real* problems—not defensively repeating partisan talking points.

I also discovered this approach is not only for chaplains or religious people. Anyone can help shape a more positive leadership culture by choosing to express gratitude and desiring the best for leaders. When more of us engage elected leaders in this way, shaping a positive leadership culture where public policy is made is possible. There is power within you, and all of us, to change the culture of our politics.

This is not only true of politics. Shaping culture through gratitude and desiring the best for leaders can happen in any environment. The people in positions of authority who think, work, and lead better are needed just as much in corporate boardrooms, schools, and in our homes and neighborhoods. Right now, however, we particularly need to shape a positive leadership culture in politics.

The Current Political Moment

It is no secret that our politics are in a bad place. We seem unable to respectfully disagree with one another, and our political discourse is marked by unyielding partisanship, hostility, and incivility. Research on the state of political polarization in the country shows that even "in a dramatically strengthening economy, more than four in ten Americans say they think the nation's best years are behind us."[2]

Tragically, we see divisiveness, hostility, and the increasingly heated tone of our politics negatively affecting opinions of the country in general. Arthur Brooks, an authority in applied microeconomics and mathematical modeling, explains that years of "political shifts, cultural change, and the uncertainties of a modern, globalized world" led to a sense of deep pessimism in America. An expert in economics and public policy, Brooks says the core problem perpetuating the sense of pessimism is not a lack of economic growth and opportunity. Rather, the problem is that Americans are living in what he calls a *culture of contempt*:

> We need national healing every bit as much as economic growth. But what are we getting instead from many of our leaders in media, politics, entertainment, and academia? Across the political spectrum, people in positions of power and influence are setting us against one another . . . In the very moment in which America most needs to come together as a nation—in the early decades of what, for the good of the world, should be a new American century—we are being torn apart.[3]

Brooks is unwilling to concede to the trajectory of a contempt culture. He presents ways to solve the problem of contempt in his book *Love Your Enemies: How Decent People Can Save America from a Culture of Contempt*. In his book, Brooks addresses the problem of contempt with careful precision and then applies those methods broadly across society. America can be saved, and the solution Brooks offers is "more love and less contempt."[4]

Disagreement and conflict are not new to politics and neither is the resulting sense of discouragement. Brooks's solution to the contempt culture isn't new either. Ancient philosophers warned of the dangers of contempt on society and for governmental leaders in particular. According to the Greek philosopher Aristotle, in *Politics*, hatred and contempt are the two things which most undermine government. Aristotle goes on to say goodwill is the opposite of hatred.[5] In *The Education of a Christian Prince*, the sixteenth-century Dutch philosopher Erasmus cites Aristotle and calls it a leader's duty to carefully cultivate goodwill and avoid contempt in society.

He writes that goodwill is fostered by "mercy, fairness, courtesy, and compassion . . . [whereas contempt is] engendered by self-indulgence, the company of fools and parasites, and also by stupidity and negligence."[6]

Brooks is right that contempt is gripping the culture of American politics, perhaps due in part to a lack of mercy, courtesy, and compassion or to an abundance of self-indulgence and negligence. Regardless of the specific social ills fueling the growing contempt, the result is a number of problems in the current political moment. Among them are the problems of incivility, disrespect, an inability to respectfully disagree, and the presence of fear in our politics.

The Problem of Incivility

It is not shocking to suggest we have an incivility problem. Research consistently finds incivility on the rise in American culture and society. Beginning in 2010, the annual Civility in America survey by Weber Shandwick, partnering with Powell Tate and KRC Research, found that more than 90 percent of those surveyed said incivility is a problem. In 2019, the survey found 68 percent said incivility was a "major problem" in the public square and identified politics as a major contributing factor to the incivility. Alarmingly, incivility leads to cyberbullying, harassment, intolerance, hate crimes, decreased community engagement, and people feeling less safe in public. Another tragic consequence of incivility is how substantial majorities think the tone of public discourse is harming America's future and are discouraging the kinds of people we need from entering public service and leadership.[7]

Incivility is not only harming political and public discourse but is also present in the workplace. Researchers Christine Porath and Christine Pearson have studied the cost of incivility in the workplace. Collecting data from more than fourteen thousand people throughout the United States and Canada, Porath and Pearson studied the prevalence, types, causes, costs, and cures of incivility at work. Polling eight hundred managers and employees in seventeen industries, they learned how people react to incivility. Their data shows nearly half (48 percent) of those surveyed intentionally decreased their work effort. A further 78 percent said their commitment to their organization declined, and 12 percent left their job because of the uncivil treatment. A quarter of those surveyed admitted to taking their frustration out on others.[8]

Porath and Pearson identified a number of discouraging consequences to incivility. First, their research showed that creativity suffers. Environments fraught with incivility resulted in people "producing 25 percent fewer ideas, and the ones they did come up with were less original." If decreased creativity is also a consequence of incivility in politics, we should expect fewer innovative solutions to real problems from political leaders when we really need more. The research also indicates people are less likely to get involved or provide help when the environment is uncivil. Again, if the same is true in politics, then we have fewer people bringing ideas, resources, and solutions.[9]

What are we to do? Obviously, we need to restore civility in America. However, to reverse the trend of growing incivility, a number of authors comment that civility is too low a bar to set. We should aspire to more than simply being nice to one another. I appreciate the sentiment but respectfully suggest working to restore civility is still a good place to start. Through their research, Porath and Pearson identify a number of strategies to break through the incivility, three of which are the very same strategies we can employ in our approach to engaging leaders.

First, begin with yourself and model good behavior. Do not respond in kind when witnessing incivility or when you are on the receiving end of it. The second strategy is to adopt a more thankful or appreciative attitude. Porath and Pearson write, "One way to help create a culture of respect . . . is to express appreciation." An attitude of thankfulness is the foundation of step two of our process for engaging leaders. Third, engage people who model respect and civility and avoid incivility to begin with.[10] We need more people of strong character and integrity entering public service and leadership. We need more—not less—creativity, innovation, and respect marking political dialogue.

The Problem of Disrespect

The Bible consistently tells us to respect leaders. This is true when discussing leaders within the community of faith. "You must not blaspheme God or curse a leader among your people."[11] The command in Exodus carries over to leaders beyond the people of God. Paul writes in Titus 3 that we should submit to rulers and governing authorities. He says the same in Romans 13, further explaining they are instruments of God tasked with punishing evil. J. Oliver Buswell writes the following in *A Systematic Theology of Christian Religion*: "The chief function of government emphasized by Paul in the thirteenth chapter of Romans is the forcible maintenance of law and order, restraining evil deeds and encouraging the good."[12]

Paul teaches Christians to honor those in authority because of their responsibility to restrain corruption, injustice, and evil. When asked about a person's responsibility to governing authorities, Jesus responded, "Give, then, to Caesar the things that are Caesar's, and to God the things that are God's."[13] Despite the Bible's clarity on respecting leaders, increased contempt and hostility toward them is commonplace. One reason for the growing inability to show respect to leaders may be a product of democracy itself.

Democracy, where the people of a nation hold the power to elect leaders, is among the greatest of human achievements. The ability to choose one's leaders is an extraordinary blessing that has not existed for most of human history and doesn't exist everywhere today. But, as with all human achievements, there can be good and bad consequences. For example, having the power to choose leaders does not guarantee the best leaders will be chosen. Further, the power to vote leaders out of office may lead to a growing inability to show respect while they serve in office. David Pawson makes this observation in his commentary on 1 and 2 Thessalonians:

> The city of Thessalonica operated with a democratic form of government. One positive result of this was . . . the degree of [freedom] that was not enjoyed elsewhere . . . But a negative result of this democratic system was that [the people] had little or no respect for their leaders.[14]

We should be careful not to take Pawson's statement too far. Scripture does not require a blind respect for leaders. There are times when leaders are so morally flawed that they lose the respect of the people they lead. There are other times when leaders impose policies that so clearly contradict biblical commands that both our conscience and convictions require us to disobey. Is it possible to disobey the legitimate authority of leaders without showing disrespect? The Book of Daniel demonstrates how someone can respectfully disagree and even disobey the ruling authorities. It is possible to disagree without disrespecting, but it's not easy and requires considerable courage.

The events recorded in the Book of Daniel take place during a time of great tragedy in the life of God's people. Generations after the nation of Israel fractured into two separate kingdoms and engaged in conflict with powerful foreign enemies, Jerusalem fell to the conquering Babylonian Empire. The invading armies forcibly captured a portion of the Jewish people and took them back to Babylon, specifically choosing members of the royal family, elders, court officials, and priests.[15] Living as exiles, the Jewish people learned the customs of their Babylonian captors and begin serving the needs and interests of the empire.

This is the situation when the Bible records the events of four Jewish captives serving in the court of King Nebuchadnezzar: Daniel, Hananiah, Mishael, and Azariah. They were given new Babylonian names: Beltehazzar, Shadrach, Meshach, and Abednego. Forced to live and serve the Babylonian empire, these four men remained faithful to live according to their Jewish faith traditions and earned the favor of both Nebuchadnezzar and Darius, who sought their counsel and gave them significant governmental responsibilities.[16]

Despite the favor each man enjoyed from the Babylonian kings, the Book of Daniel records two significant conflicts leading Daniel, Shadrach, Meshach, and Abednego to disobey. Both conflicts center around a particular policy that egregiously infringed upon their faith convictions. In one instance, the king enacts a policy requiring every person in the empire to bow down and worship a golden statue. To do so would break the first and second laws recorded in the Ten Commandments by which the people were not to have other gods or to bow down in worship to idols.[17]

The second conflict developed when wicked and conniving advisors convinced the king to sign a royal edict prohibiting any person to pray to any god or man other than the king himself. Daniel was a man of great faith and regular prayer. He is described as praying in his home three times each day. Knowing this was Daniel's practice and jealous of his influence and favor with the king, the wicked advisors crafted this edict with the sole intent of compromising Daniel and forcing his execution.

Where the first conflict involved a policy ordering the performance of a specific task, this second conflict was a prohibition of a certain activity: prayer to God. In both cases, the leaders and the laws constituted an unconscionable infringement upon the faith convictions and conscience of Daniel, Shadrach, Meshach, and Abednego.

There are six lessons about respect we can learn from Daniel and his compatriots who faced these leaders and their policies.

First, these men never compromised their convictions and acted in a manner consistent with their own conscience. When ordered to bow down and worship a golden statue representing the multiple Babylonian gods, Shadrach, Meshach, and Abednego respond by saying, "We want you as king to know that we will not serve your gods or worship the gold statue you set up."[18] When nefarious actors convinced King Darius to sign a written edict prohibiting prayer to any god or man other than the king, Daniel continued his faith practice of praying to God. We read in Daniel 6:10, "When Daniel learned that the document had been signed, he went into his house ... and three times a day he got down on his knees, prayed, and gave thanks to his God, just as he had done before." Whether ordered by law to perform a specific task or refrain from certain activities, Daniel and his compatriots disobeyed the reigning authorities to maintain their religious conviction.

Second, these men never denied the legitimate authority of the Babylonian kings to enact the compromising policies. In the case of Daniel, the circumstances leading to the prohibition on prayer were maliciously devised to bring harm only to him. Nevertheless, Daniel did not question the king's right to sign such an edict but appealed to God in prayer and thereby committed the specific act prohibited by law. In the case of Shadrach, Meshach, and Abednego, they tell Nebuchadnezzar, "[God] can rescue us from the power of you, the king," thereby acknowledging the power of the king to punish their disobedience by throwing them into a fiery furnace to be burned alive.[19]

Third, resolved they could not in good conscience obey the policies enacted by the governing authority, Daniel, Shadrach, Meshach, and Abednego each made a personal decision to disobey. They did not form alliances or mount public campaigns against the damning policies. Neither did they seek to delegitimize the authority of the king. Granted, Shadrach, Meshach, and Abednego stood together when refusing to bow down to the golden statue, but there is no indication their defiance was anything other than a personal decision each of them made.

Fourth, these men were willing to pay the penalty for their disobedience and in both instances the penalty was certain death. Daniel was thrown into a den of hungry lions while Shadrach, Meshach, and Abednego were cast into a blazing furnace. Civil disobedience is most compelling when people suffer the known consequences for defying unjust policies. It was not only the content of Martin Luther King Jr.'s strategy of nonviolent resistance to racism but also defending his strategy in an open letter from jail that so effectively challenged the evil permeating the American South. King writes, "We were not unmindful of the difficulties involved . . . [and] repeatedly asked ourselves the questions, 'Are you able to accept blows without retaliating?' and 'Are you able to endure the ordeals of jail?'"[20] Whether a royal edict in ancient Babylon or unjust Jim Crow laws in Alabama circa 1963, these men were willing to suffer the consequences for disobeying unjust laws. This is a hard lesson to learn because no one should have to suffer the consequences of unjust laws. That is exactly why some do and what makes their courage and sacrifice all the more inspiring and important.

Fifth, when facing the consequences for their disobedience, Daniel and his compatriots never stopped trusting God. Nebuchadnezzar's questioning of Shadrach, Meshach, and Abednego is one of the most dramatic exchanges between the people of God and a hostile governing leader recorded in history. Nebuchadnezzar is repeatedly described as being filled with furious rage when questioning the three men and warning them the punishment for refusing to bow down to the golden statue was to be thrown into a fiery furnace. The three responded to the king:

If the God we serve exists, then he can rescue us from the furnace of blazing fire, and he can rescue us from the power of you, the king. But even if he does not rescue us, we want you as king to know that we will not serve your gods or worship the gold statue you set up.[21]

Their unwavering trust in God gave each man the courage to face the consequences of disobeying the king. Their steadfast trust in God and courage echoed across history in three words, often quoted as "and if not." These words inspired one of the most extraordinary events at a consequential moment during World War II when Hitler's armies seemed poised to wipe out the beleaguered British Expeditionary Forces cornered against the sea at Dunkirk, France. Charles Colson tells the remarkable story like this:

But as the British people waited anxiously, a three-word message was transmitted from the army at Dunkirk: "And if not."

The British people instantly recognized what the message meant: "Even if we are not rescued from Hitler's army, we will stand strong." [The phrase] "And if not" was found in the Book of Daniel, where Shadrach, Meshach, and Abednego defied Nebuchadnezzar, putting their trust in God.

The message galvanized the British people. Thousands of boats set out across the Channel in a gallant bid to rescue their army. And they succeeded. Nearly 350,000 troops were saved.[22]

The sixth and final lesson to learn from the Book of Daniel is that even when choosing to disobey, neither Daniel nor Shadrach, Meshach, and Abednego ever disrespected the king. To the contrary, the text demonstrates time and again that Daniel and his compatriots were consistent in showing respect. When facing an enraged Nebuchadnezzar and knowing their response was not what he wanted to hear, Shadrach, Meshach, and Abednego voiced their unwillingness to comply with the king's wishes while humbly submitting to the king's stated consequences.

When the stone was removed from the lion's den and King Darius cried out to see if Daniel was alive, Daniel responded in the custom of those who address the king, calling out, "May the king live forever." Daniel then explained how God protected him from the lions because he was innocent before God, "and also before you, Your Majesty, I have not done harm."[23] We learn from the Book of Daniel that it is possible to disagree and even disobey governing authorities without showing disrespect.

The Problem of Disagreement

Few situations can be more uncomfortable than interacting with someone we disagree with, particularly when the disagreement is over politics. According to the University of California at Berkley's Bridging Differences Initiative, which explores evidence-based practices to improve dialogue, understanding, and relationships across social and political issues, "Even simple disagreements can make us uncomfortable. That might be why Americans are increasingly segregating into like-minded communities."[24] These communities can be in-person relationships or online forums for social and political dialogue that often operate like echo chambers where we become vulnerable to the effects of confirmation bias and lack the ability to look at things objectively.

Alternatively, talking to people we disagree with can help increase our own objectivity and cause us to think more deeply about our political behavior, positions, or opinions. There can also be other benefits to engaging with people we disagree with, rather than avoiding them. We can practice greater empathy and learn to better understand the circumstances and experiences that frame opposing positions or points of view. We also become more comfortable and skilled in navigating difficult discussions over complex ideas or issues.

Finally, and perhaps obviously, talking to people we don't agree with reminds us that we simply do not always agree with each other. But we also remember that we are not supposed to. The blessing of living in a representative democracy is how individual leaders are chosen to speak for the needs and interests of their respective communities or legislative districts. These communities offer unique perspectives and resources but also have different needs and challenges. There are times when the needs and political positions of various communities will align with one another, but there are also times when they have conflicting or competing interests. When those areas of disagreement surface, we should remember that politics is not a zero-sum game. Any political progress of today stands on the shoulders of past policy decisions. What is more, there will be future elections and legislative sessions where new leaders will write new laws. One of the clearest distinctions between politics and the gospel is this: politics says, *there is always tomorrow,* whereas the gospel says, *it is finished.*

The key is learning to endure the tension of disagreement without disrespecting one another. Respectfully engaging those leaders who were elected to represent the diverse communities, perspectives, and points of view can be hard to do, especially when we don't agree with them. It's hard because we trust too much in politics, governments, institutions, and people. We are trusting in things that can inevitably let us down. It is too easy to become comfortable and live like this world is all there is. If we are honest, we have made an idol out of our politics, and it's tearing our nation apart. Tim Keller helps us to know when we have made an idol of politics:

> One of the signs that an object is functioning as an idol is
> that fear becomes one of the chief characteristics of life. If
> our counterfeit god is threatened in any way, our response

is complete panic. We do not say, 'What a shame, how difficult,' but rather 'This is the end! There's no hope!' This may be a reason why so many people now respond to U.S. political trends in such an extreme way. When either party wins an election, a certain percentage of the losing side talks openly about leaving the country. They become agitated and fearful for the future. They have put the kind of hope in their political leaders and policies that once was reserved for God and the work of the gospel.[25]

I'm afraid Keller has assessed our society correctly. We have made an idol of our politics, but we are in good company. The Apostle Paul made an idol of his politics too. He trusted exclusively in his religious and political structure and was so entirely dependent on the politics of the Mosaic Law as a Pharisee that he reacted with ferocious fear and anger when his idol of religious nationalism was challenged. Paul became an extremist when challenged by this group of Christ-followers, and it drove him to brutality and persecution.

Paul's assumptions of the gospel kept him from considering what it actually claimed. Instead, he projected worst expectations on those who disagreed with him, naming them enemies. That sounds very similar to the current political discourse in our country. While traveling to Damascus to drive out the Christians he saw as his opponents, Paul encountered the actual claims of the gospel. Chapter 4 will discuss in greater detail how this encounter transformed Paul's perspective.

How Paul viewed world events, institutions, religions, empires, and the ultimate source of authority itself forever changed after encountering the actual claims of the gospel. He completely transformed from the hostile, combative, and divisive figure he formerly was. The once brutal antagonist who perpetuated fear and hate became an effective proponent of grace and forgiveness, breaking down societal boundaries and crossing political, philosophical, and racial boundaries. Isn't that precisely what we want to see in our current cultural moment? The capacity to change is possible, and the same people fueling hostility and division can yet become the very peacemakers and bridge builders bringing diverse groups and differing points of view together.

The Problem of Fear in Our Politics

When recently attending a leadership forum in Washington DC, I visited with two members of the US House of Representatives, one Republican and one Democrat. Early in our discussion, the congressmen commented that a few characteristics routinely emerge in many of their political discussions. Many people they talk to voice frustration, anger, resentment, and fear.

One of the current problems in American politics is fear, according to a host of articles, commentators, academics, and former President Jimmy Carter. Addressing the Carter Center's Human Rights Defenders Forum in 2016, President Carter said, "What is needed now, more than ever, is leadership that steers us away from fear and fosters greater confidence in the inherent goodness and ingenuity of humanity."[26] It seems that every time I listen to a political interview or news story, someone typically raises the subject of fear. What are we so afraid of? Some stories suggest people fear for their safety and fear threats to their freedom, economic stability, or access to health care. Others are afraid they are losing the country and society they love.

I reject the idea that American democracy is fragile and believe it is extraordinarily resilient. However, democracy is vulnerable, and fear is perhaps the greatest threat. During a 2018 *PBS NewsHour* interview, Martha Nussbaum, professor at the University of Chicago and author of *The Monarchy of Fear,* a book exploring the 2016 election, said, "Fear connects us to the bad . . . [and] it's always been thought to be a terrible problem for democracy." Professor Nussbaum goes on to say, "When fear gets into the works . . . [it] makes us turn against targets that are not real . . . People are being stampeded by their emotions and they're not stopping to figure things out and to work on the real problems."[27]

At various times, political leaders confront the problem of fear in politics. In a world filled with danger, President Franklin Roosevelt famously said, "The only thing we have to fear is fear itself." Delivered in his first inaugural address, these words lifted the spirits of a country in the grips of the Great Depression and this statement remained an enduring legacy of President Roosevelt's leadership of a nation going to war and marshalling the courage of millions who would fight. Theirs would be later called the Greatest Generation in American history. Regrettably, his encouragement faded. Fear again grips our nation, at least when it comes to politics. We need lasting solutions to fear and not just momentary help from political leadership.

The Bible's answer to fear begins with trusting God and drawing near to His presence: "Haven't I commanded you: be strong and courageous? Do not be afraid or discouraged, for the Lord your God is with you wherever you go."[28] The writers of the New Testament teach that God's presence is closer than we imagine because God's Spirit dwells within us.[29] The Bible then teaches that fear itself is driven out by love: "There is no fear in love. But perfect love drives out fear."[30] The key is understanding how perfect love works.

The Apostle Paul writes that God's Spirit brings many things into a Christian's life, beginning with love. When I encounter a person who is difficult to love, even someone who angrily disagrees with me, I am not left to find it within myself to somehow respond with love. Love is not some mysterious substance I possess by being strong or well-adjusted enough. Love exists outside of me, first of all in the very nature of God.

God says you can debate the person in political opposition to you with civility and compassion. Love is not arrogant, boastful, rude, or self-seeking. God says you can forgive the person who wrongs you *just* as you were forgiven. Love keeps no records of wrongs.[31] When Paul writes that the fruit of the Spirit is love, he means for me to know that God provides the love I need to show. This is true in politics and everyday life. It seems there is much politics can gain from the Christian faith and the wisdom found in the Bible.

The Problem of Mixing Faith and Politics

Much is said about the role faith ought to play in politics. Since the 2016 election, public perception of the relationship between evangelical Christianity and politics has become increasingly complicated, to say the least. Christians may feel uneasy about engaging in politics, perhaps out of a desire to avoid being drawn into the minutia of policy debates or caught in the crossfire of toxic dialogue. Even with the best intentions, talking politics has a way of going sideways. If our political culture is bad now, why risk potentially making it worse?

However, Christians have no reason to give in to fear if the solution to fear is perfect love. The Bible teaches that God himself *is* love[32] and resides in the heart of every Christian. Driving out fear so we can address *the real problems* should be exactly what Christians bring to politics. We need reasonable people of faith participating in politics.

We read in 1 John 4:11-12, "Dear friends, if God loved us in this way, we also must love one another. No one has ever seen God." However, John teaches, "If we love one another, God remains in us and his love is made complete in us." The unseen is made visible at any moment, and you don't have to wait for it; it's waiting for you to love another person. Fear in politics can be driven out and replaced by the very face of God when the people of God, filled with the Spirit of God, show the love of God.

Leading Us Forward

Like Arthur Brooks, I also believe America can be saved and there is a path out of the incivility, vitriol, and increasingly partisan mentality that is dominating our political discourse. Where Brooks focuses on society at large, I challenge you to intentionally look first to leaders themselves. There are three steps to the approach for how civility, integrity, and the leaders we need are possible. The first step is *believing* leaders matter. This is more than just another way of saying, "Elections have consequences." Chapter 2 will explore how believing leaders matter is more than an intellectual understanding of the nature of authority. Believing leaders matter demands that we think of leaders as people and resist the tendency to reduce leaders to nothing more than a caricature of the political party or policies they promote.

When we remember that leaders are people just like you and me, we become more compassionate to the everyday struggles and challenges that we all have. Then we can move on to step two of the process: asking more *for* leaders. This means desiring the best for them as a person. We should desire that our leaders are healthy. We need to remember our leaders have families and other responsibilities beyond their public trust. Just as we hope for our own lives, we should desire our leader's homes are safe and filled with joy. I will encourage you to begin praying for your leaders, but prayer is not the only method. Whatever method you choose, asking more *for* leaders develops an even greater ability to think of leaders as people. The distance between the person and their position grows.

Believing leaders matter and asking more *for* them takes you to the third step of this process: asking more *of* leaders. America can get past the incivility plaguing our politics and popular culture, but we need leaders who will get us there. We need leaders who reject the tired political narratives and unhelpful partisan appeals. We need leaders who know in their hearts that they are the ones who establish culture by setting the tone. That is true in any organization or community, from the family to civic and religious organizations to private companies and whole industries.

Having the ambition to change culture is exhilarating and daunting. Where do we begin? Look first at the people serving in leadership positions at the state and local level. Look at mayors, county judges, state legislators, and your governor. We can and should ask more of leaders, but we must also look to ourselves. True, leaders are vested with the necessary power and authority that governs society and moves us forward. But leaders do not emerge from a vacuum. Culture produces its leaders. Let's not only focus on the leaders we currently have but also begin teaching, modeling, and instilling in ourselves the values and qualities we want in future leaders.

This means that asking more of leaders may not be quite what you think. There are responsibilities we expect our leaders to perform, and we hold them accountable when they fail to do so. We are blessed to live in a representative democracy where we choose our leaders. There are also policies that matter to us, and we should participate in the political process to advocate for the principles and policies we believe are best.

However, if we truly desire civility and integrity in our country, then we should think about values and characteristics that mark such leaders. Chapters 9-13 will explore nine virtues we need in leaders and ourselves. Finally, we need to think better about the nature of authority itself. What gives political leaders their authority and power? What power do we have? How we answer these questions shapes the leadership culture, changing the way we engage leaders, and can transform the tone of our politics altogether. We can pursue more productive methods for engaging with leaders, but we cannot ignore and should not forfeit the power we have. Political participation and advocacy take many forms, and we should consider which approaches are best to promote the culture we desire in our politics.

The objective of this book is to develop a thoughtful and practical approach to the problem of incivility, particularly in our political discourse. I don't believe America's best days are behind us. I do believe the civility, integrity, and leaders we need are possible. Getting there will take an intentional focus upon leaders themselves.

Believe leaders matter.

Ask more *for* leaders.

Ask more *of* leaders.

Chapter 2

★ ★ ★ ★ ★

When Making Your Voice Heard

Heroic leadership is not simply a quality or entity possessed by someone; it is a type of relationship between leader and led.

—James MacGregor Burns[1]

The Possible

Shaping a more positive culture of civility, integrity, and servant leadership among policymakers is the ultimate goal of my work. That is a lofty and needed goal in our individual states and entire nation these days. Is it really possible? What difference can my voice really make? Those questions are not helpful. In our hearts, we know that representative democracy is a gift that should not be squandered. Our voices matter, and we want to get involved in the political process guiding our country, but the heated tone of our politics is alarming. Perhaps it is best not to get involved. That may seem wise if you don't want to get drawn into contentious debates and the frequently toxic dialogue.

I feel the same way at times but also believe the civility, integrity, and leaders we need are possible, so I must make my voice heard—and not just my voice but many. All reasonable people can agree civility is needed and worth our shared effort to attain. It will require reasonable people on all sides of the issues—conservatives and liberals across the political spectrum—and from all walks of life to be willing to ask for more. We must then choose to do what we can to promote the civility and respect we want to see.

For Christians who participate in politics, however, being civil and promoting a respectful and gracious dialogue is not a choice but a command. Concerning their relationship with governing authorities, Paul writes to the church in Crete, "Remind them to submit to rulers and authorities, to obey, to be ready for every good work, to slander no one, to avoid fighting, and to be kind, always showing gentleness to all people."[2] There is no mistaking the apostle's instruction for how the Christian faith informs your public and political life. It is clearly a command, but being civil in politics is also an opportunity to demonstrate respectful dialogue in the midst of disagreement. By their own example, Christians should disrupt hostility with grace and drive out the fear getting in the way of fruitful debate in politics. Bruce Ashford and Heath Thomas call this grace-fueled civility:

> [It is] imperative for Christians is to be civil in our public demeanor. Amid the West's toxic public square, Christians' political interactions should stand out from the fray. Our public speech and political actions should reveal the difference Christ makes when he takes lordship of our lives. As representatives of Christ the King, we must combine grace and truth by being convictional and civil. Without conviction, we will be public wimps. Without grace-fueled civility, we will be yet another political loudmouth or bully.[3]

Through such grace-fueled civility, Christians demonstrate the deep substance of their faith. They can certainly regret the tone and toxicity of political discourse in the nation without despairing or losing hope. Light seems to shine the brightest when the darkness is overwhelming. Being civil through the simplest acts of kindness and respectful words is a stark contrast to the incivility and a breath of fresh air. But the goal is to promote civility beyond the behavior of any one individual involved in politics.

The verses in Titus 3:1-2 indicate Christians have a personal responsibility to model civility through showing gentleness to all people, being kind, and avoiding fights. Yet, these statements come after the reminder to submit to rulers and authorities, obey, and be ready for every good work. One conclusion might be that our own behavior and actions can bring civility into the public square but promoting civility across public discourse is accomplished through the way we respect, interact, and engage with leaders.

The process outlined in this book is just one approach for engaging leaders and breaking through the incivility in our politics. But it is one approach that all kinds of people can implement. Thankfulness and desiring the best for leaders are keys for effectiveness as a chaplain to political leaders and the foundation of the process for engaging leaders presented in this book. While thankfulness and desiring the best for leaders are obvious methods for a chaplain, anyone can engage leaders with this process.

What if you seem to be the only one trying? That is another less-than-helpful question for those wanting to shape a positive leadership culture, and there is good news. You're not the only one. There are many working to elevate the tone of our politics, but they don't get as much press as they should, and many are working behind the scenes. There is more good news. I have seen how this approach does make a difference, even when it is just one person who is committed to the goal of shaping a positive leadership culture. That is the reason for putting this approach into the book you are now reading. You can make a difference, and this three-step process is a place to start. More will join us, and along the way, I believe you will begin meeting others who are already involved.

Together, we can navigate out of the incivility and see our country aspire to the heights of progress, political debate, and policy innovation we know are possible in America. The first step is *believing leaders matter*. When we believe leaders matter and engage them with an attitude of thankfulness and desiring the best for them, it will transform the political and policy-making culture.

Three Reasons Leaders Matter

Labelling the first step of the process as *believing leaders matter* assumes that not everyone agrees they do. Believing leaders matter comes easily to me because I have always aspired to be a leader. That is probably true of you or anyone reading a book entitled *When Leaders Matter*. We are students of leadership. Speaking for myself, I cannot help but see the leadership dynamic in every situation. There are good leaders who are strong and inspire those they lead and transformational leaders who see a better future and motivate the people they lead to achieve it. There are also bad leaders who frustrate and discourage the people they lead. There are overreaching leaders and micro-managers. There can also be the worst of situations: absent leaders who create a leadership vacuum and leave people wondering who is in charge.

While not an exhaustive list, here are three reasons to believe leaders matter: first, we have interest and fascination with leadership and leaders; second, many possess the desire to become leaders; and third, leaders matter because they possess and exercise authority.

1. The Fascination with Leadership and Leaders

The research, scholarship, and expertise dedicated to understanding leadership dynamics, situations, qualities, and theories is immense. The first argument for why leaders matter could be a simple appeal to the sheer volume of published work on the subject of leaders and leadership. A basic internet search using the question, "How many books on leadership exist?" directed me to an article from Michael Shinagel, the dean of the Division of Continuing Education and University Extension at Harvard University. Shinagel writes, "According to a recent survey, there are more than 15,000 books on leadership in print. Articles on leadership number in the thousands each year." That is a lot of time, talent, and ink devoted to the subject of leaders. Shinagel continues, "The obvious conclusions we can draw from these facts are that there are more books and articles on leadership available than we can ever hope to read and that leadership clearly is a crucial and abiding topic of interest to countless women and men in society."[4]

I am one of many grateful beneficiaries of those writers and thinkers. Even though the number of leadership books in my library is more than I have read, the leadership section is always the first place I go in any bookstore. I am not the only one drawn to read and learn more about leadership. In his book *Conviction to Lead*, Albert Mohler writes, "When you find a leader, you have found a reader. The reason is this simple—there is no substitute for effective reading when it comes to developing and maintaining the intelligence necessary to lead."[5]

If you are reading this book, the chances are probably good that you already agree leaders matter. It's likely you are the sort of person Mohler has in mind as well. When it comes to the subject of leadership, there are those of us who never stop learning and reading, which is encouraging when considering the question of whether or not leaders matter.

More than the overwhelming interest in the subject of leadership, we are fascinated with leaders themselves. Visit the leadership section of your local bookstore and find the many biographies of leaders on the shelf—from presidents and generals to captains of industry and pioneers in innovation and research. The latest leadership book on my reading list is by Stanley McChrystal, Jeff Eggers, and Jason Mangone, entitled *Leaders: Myth and Reality*. In it, the authors evaluate the nature of leadership by profiling thirteen individual leaders, from Robert E. Lee, Albert Einstein, and Martin Luther King Jr., to Walt Disney, Margaret Thatcher, and Coco Chanel.

The fascination with leaders also extends to those we consider morally evil—or at least on the wrong side of history. In addition to Robert E. Lee, the authors of *Leaders: Myth and Reality* also profiled the al-Qaeda leader, Abu Musab Al-Zarqawi, one of General McChrystal's primary military targets in the Iraqi theater. As the authors point out, "Leadership itself is neither good nor evil. Malevolent leaders emerge with surprising frequency, as often as those we judge to be good. Leadership is better judged as either effective or not."[6] To understand leaders, McChrystal and his co-authors follow the example of first-century Greek writer Plutarch, who "wrote ancient biography, not history . . . [and] was more interested in the question 'What sort of man was he?' rather than 'What did he do?'"[7]

The interest in leadership and leaders suggests leaders do matter, but the fascination comes with a warning as well: "Here lies the root cause of the mythology of leadership—its relentless focus on the leader."[8] In *Leaders: Myth and Reality*, McChrystal and his co-authors suggest that solely focusing on the leaders themselves leads to a wrong belief that the success of one leader can be replicated in another. We should learn from leaders but need to reject certain myths developed by our fascination with leaders.

We can wrongly believe leadership is a formula to be followed or that a leader's success can always be attributed to the characteristics and actions of the person in charge. We neglect the organization surrounding people in leadership. "We're led to believe that leadership is what the leader does, but in reality, outcomes are attributable to far more than the individual leader."[9] McChrystal concludes that leadership is more than the person in charge and the outcomes we see: "[Leadership] is equally concerned with how complex human groups optimize their cooperation and how individuals find symbols of meaning and purpose in life."[10]

These symbols of meaning that give purpose in life are also driving our toxic political culture. Look no further than the headlines dominating traditional media and social media threads for the evidence this is true. On a rare and refreshing occasion, the media will just report the political news. Mostly, the political events of the hour are relentlessly scrutinized and editorialized. Pundits play to our worst fears and escalate the severity of every political event. Then, we begin hearing the familiar catchphrase every two and four years that the next election is "the most important election of our lifetime." If you believe that is true, then you also believe leaders matter.

2. The Desire to Lead

Another reason that leaders matter is in the *desire to lead*. Al Mohler writes in *Conviction to Lead*, "[Real] leaders . . . are passionate about leadership. They are tired of seeing organizations and movements die or decline, and they want to change things for the better."[11] Not everyone in positions of leadership is ready to lead or effective in their leadership. Nevertheless, the desire to effect change and solve problems manifests as aspiring to be a leader.

One of my favorite questions to ask of an elected official is this: "What was the thing, moment, or belief that put you over the edge when you decided to run—to put yourself and your family through the rigors of a campaign?" The answers are as numerous as the legislators themselves. In each and every instance, I notice a story of struggle, trial, testing, and endurance, coupled with a genuine feeling that they were called to run.

I've listened to many legislators describe how humbling and exhilarating it is when the desire to lead results in their attaining positions of leadership. But leadership takes a toll. "People who lead frequently bear scars from their efforts to bring about . . . change" because the reality is, "leaders are always failing somebody."[12] The internal passion, drive, motivation, and sense of calling are never more needed than at those decisive moments in leadership where some walk away satisfied and others not.

3. The Power and Authority of Leaders

Third, and most compellingly, leaders matter because they possess and exercise real authority. The Bible specifically acknowledges the existence of governmental authority in Romans 13:1: "Let everyone submit to the governing authorities, since there is no authority except from God, and the authorities that exist are instituted by God." Jesus affirmed that governmental leaders possess authority when standing before Pontius Pilate:

> So Pilate said to him, "Do you refuse to speak to me? Don't you know that I have the authority to release you and the authority to crucify you?"
>
> "You *would* have no authority over me at all," Jesus answered him, *"if it hadn't been given you* from above."[13]

The reality of a leader's power and authority cannot be understated and lies at the very heart of why I wrote this book. Understanding the nature of authority is critical to believing leaders matter. Harvard Business Professor Ronald Heifetz writes in his book *Leadership Without Easy Answers,* "Social living depends on authority. Indeed, our capacity to form authority relationships lies at the base of our organizations, from the family to the nation."[14]

Heifetz describes a social contract between the members of a society and the leaders holding positions of authority. As with any contract, there are responsibilities. Leaders must fulfill certain expectations, and there are consequences when leaders fall short in meeting those expectations or do not effectively perform needed functions. Heifetz explains, "We expect decisive direction, protection, orientation, control of conflict and the restoration of norms. We expect authorities to step into the breach . . . to restore equilibrium."[15]

In this contract, leaders are empowered and entrusted to exercise that power in ways that serve society as a whole. In this way, authority becomes a resource for effective leadership in a society in a number of important ways. Leaders have the ability to *command and direct our attention*. Whether through campaigns, speeches, or legislative sessions, political leaders set the policy agenda and also have the *power to frame issues* when crafting public policy. Further, leaders have *access to information* and a certain level of *control over the flow of information*. Finally, leaders have the power to choose the *decision-making process*.[16] This is true of governmental leaders as well as leaders in local communities, private companies, and all sorts of institutions.

With all the resources and the power that comes through authority, leaders naturally become the focus of our attention when things don't go well. The current national moment seems marked by conflict, with growing social unrest, competition over resources, clashing political and economic philosophies, and injustices of various kinds. These aren't small problems. They are complex, and finding effective solutions requires serious deliberation that incorporates a range of perspectives, skill, and wisdom. Solving these problems will take a host of leaders from diverse backgrounds and experiences who are able to bring all their skill and insight to the table. Make no mistake. Now is the time to address *real* problems and challenges. This is also what I mean by asking more *of* leaders.

Don't Give Your Power Away

It is important to remember there is a difference between leadership and authority. Heifetz says we intuitively know this is true. He explains that even though "we often equate leadership with authority . . . and we routinely call [those who achieve positions of authority] leaders, on reflection, we readily acknowledge the frequent lack of leadership they provide."[17]

According to the social contract Heifetz suggests, we look to our leaders to solve problems. We still look to our leaders when they do not succeed, if now only because we believe the solution must be replacing them. After all, while our contract with leaders grants them certain authority, the power to remove that authority stays with us. But the current culture of incivility, vitriol, and blind partisanship in American politics is invoking a predictable response. Every two and four years we hear the same things:

"We need new leaders."

"Those in power can't solve our problems."

"The current administration is causing our problems."

"This is the most important election of our lifetime!"

The continuous cycle of replacing leaders is not solving our incivility problem. Let me be clear. I am in no way saying elections are not important. There are leaders who lack the integrity we demand. These are certainly times when new leadership is needed and the most appropriate response to what happens in our country is electing new leaders. But what has this pattern produced? The pendulum swings, and new leaders take over. What about the social unrest? Rather than dissipating, we sense it growing more intense and entrenched into an increasingly divisive and stratified culture.

There is an even more alarming trend developing in recent years. The common response to newly elected leaders is to make every effort to delegitimize them. When a new person or party assumes power, rather than working to address the issues raised during a campaign, their first priority becomes establishing a sense of their own legitimacy. Wasn't that the purpose of elections?

The ability to remove and replace those in authority is becoming the primary expression of the power held by society. The evidence of this is our growing hyper-focus on elections and making leaders the scapegoats we blame for our problems. Heifetz calls our tendency toward looking too much to leaders for solutions maladaptive:

> Habitually seeking solutions from people in authority is maladaptive . . . The flight to authority is particularly dangerous for at least two reasons: first, because the work avoidance often occurs in response to our biggest problems and, second, because it disables some of our most important personal and collective resources.[18]

Perhaps the real problem is that we have misunderstood the conditions of our contract with leaders. Leaders do matter when addressing the problems of society, but so do all the people they are leading. When we believe our only power comes at election time, we forfeit the authority within each of us to address big problems and face our more pressing challenges. We should not give that power away. Making your voice heard doesn't only happen at the ballot box. You can engage leaders today, whether or not you agree with them or voted for them.

Believing leaders matter results in a reclamation of your own authority and voice. With that comes the power to shape a positive leadership culture that breaks through the incivility. If restoring respect and integrity to political discourse is what you are willing to do with your voice, it will require at least two things: a strategy and a different perspective.

Chapter 3

★ ★ ★ ★ ★

When We Need a Strategy

The essence of strategy is choosing what not to do.

—Michael Porter[1]

The Political Culture We Really Want

Peace, productive dialogue, and confidence in the future is what the majority of Americans want. This was demonstrated in a 2018 study of political attitudes by More in Common, an international initiative working to "build communities and societies that are stronger, more united and more resilient to the increasing threats of polarization and social division."[2] The study showed 93 percent of Americans report they are tired of how divided the country has become, with 71 percent indicating they believe this "strongly." The study also found "large majorities of people believe in the importance of compromise, reject the absolutism of the extreme wings of both parties, and are not motivated by partisan loyalty."[3]

How do we reconcile the pervasive incivility and contempt with data showing the overwhelming majority of Americans desire compromise? Arthur Brooks points to two culprits. For one, Brooks believes we are addicted to contempt. If that is true, then we need look no further than ourselves to assign blame. Brooks goes on to suggest there exists what he calls an "outrage industrial complex" that "profits handsomely from our contempt addiction." Brooks explains it further:

> This starts by catering to just one ideological side. Leaders and media on the left and right then keep their audiences hooked on contempt by telling audiences what they want to hear, selling a narrative of conflict and painting gross caricatures of the other side. They make us feel justified in our own beliefs while affirming our worst assumptions about those who disagree with us.[4]

Brooks believes we need to be aware of our own complicity, as well as notice the external actors and influencers who are insidiously fueling the contempt we feel. We need a better perspective on developing events and the less-than-balanced political commentary that follows them. We also need the inner strength, thoughtfulness, and self-control that comes with a new perspective. These are the tools allowing us to rise above our own baser instincts, resist the external forces seeking to enrage and divide us, and see through tired political narratives.

Change is difficult to achieve and takes time. The time and difficultly increase when the goal is to change culture. Despite all our progress, human nature has not changed all that much, and many of the solutions to rescue America from a contempt culture that Brooks offers are rooted in ancient philosophy, wisdom, and the religious teachings from Jesus Christ, Judaism, and Buddhism. We will come back to some of these solutions in Chapter 5.

What We Need Is a Strategy

Like Brooks, I also look to sources of ancient wisdom to find models for creating positive and lasting influence. Difficult though it may be, changing the culture is possible, and history is filled with examples we should consider when developing a strategy for today. My favorite example is the Apostle Paul, the once persecutor turned leader and martyr in the earliest days of the Christian movement. Paul's mission and strategy launched a movement that transformed the world.

You might think my intentions are to continue Paul's particular mission of Christian evangelism, but it is not. I do share Paul's passion and belief, but my specific goal is to apply his strategy in such a way to shape a better leadership culture, specifically in our politics. This is good for everyone, regardless of religious belief and political ideology.

Nevertheless, I unashamedly base this approach on the strategies and principles found in the Bible. We are wise to look to authorities beyond ourselves to find solutions, especially in days of bitter disagreement. In the Bible, we find ancient wisdom that benefits all of us, whether or not you adopt the theological implications and religious beliefs claimed in it.

The wisdom guiding this approach to engaging leaders is found in portions from two of Paul's letters: his letter to the church in Rome and his first letter to Timothy in Ephesus. First, know that Paul did believe that everyday people had the power to shape the culture. Paul writes to the churches in first century Rome, "For I am not ashamed of the gospel, because it is the power of God for salvation to everyone who believes."[5] Through the unique power of the gospel, Paul believed change was possible in the heart and mind of any person. He further believed change was possible for whole communities, the broader culture, and the future of civilization itself.

Set aside your particular beliefs about the nature of the gospel for a moment, along with the associations with religion and the Christian faith in particular. Just consider the implications of Paul's life and work. He believed this message was true and powerful and could positively influence people and culture. To that end, Paul's writings show the depth of his conviction, his care for the people he worked with, and the skill with which he made use of every resource at his disposal. To say it another way, Paul had passion, a deep belief in his mission, and the conviction that what he was doing was right. Second, Paul surrounded himself with friends and partners who shared his conviction and worked together to accomplish their goal. Third, Paul had sufficient knowledge of the places he went and the people he encountered; he understood their way of life.

Elements of Paul's Strategy

Paul had something more: a strategy. He was strategic in where he preached, planted churches, and developed leaders. The first element of Paul's strategy was the *place*. He picked leading cities, places of social, governmental, philosophical, and religious influence. Paul chose key cities along trade routes of economic significance. These were places where the people responsible for leading Rome lived and worked. William Barclay writes Paul had the *eye of a strategist*:

> When Paul chose a place in which to preach the gospel, he always did so with the eye of a strategist. He always chose one which was not only important in itself but was also the key point of the whole area . . . These colonies were the focal points of the great Roman road system . . . They were founded to keep the peace and to command the strategic centers in Rome's far flung empire.[6]

The second element of his strategy was the *people*. Paul focused on leaders. Understanding the religious and philosophical culture of the places where he went and worked, Paul skillfully navigated the nuanced political and economic environments of the first-century

Roman colonies and gained an audience with governing officials throughout the empire. Paul chose shrewdly where to establish churches because he believed the gospel brings the redeeming power of God, the transforming power of truth, and the healing power of grace. He knew if this redeeming, transforming, and healing power could reach leaders, then it would help many.

The third element of Paul's strategy was his *attitude*. Specifically, Paul adopted an attitude of thankfulness for leaders and committed to pray for them. We find this in 1 Timothy 2:1-2 when Paul instructs Timothy and the church in Ephesus to pray for leaders with thanksgiving and to intercede on their behalf. As the next chapter will explore in greater detail, adopting an attitude of thankfulness and asking God to bless leaders is very difficult, especially when we don't agree with them. Keep in mind, the leaders in Paul's day were actively marginalizing, persecuting, and executing the people reading his letters. How difficult was it to adopt an attitude of thankfulness for them? But remember, Jesus taught his followers to "love your enemies and pray for those who persecute you."[7] The best way to genuinely adopt an attitude of thankfulness and pray for leaders is to intentionally set aside political agendas, no matter how good, God-honoring, or biblically consistent they may be. Be thankful for leaders and pray for God to bless them—with no other agenda.

Leaders Are Chosen Servants

The Bible leads me to believe that our political leaders are, in fact, *chosen servants*. They are democratically chosen by the people but also of God's sovereign will. This does not mean that every person elected is morally good. This also does not mean that every person elected to lead is necessarily the most qualified or skilled person for the job. To say political leaders are chosen servants means that in every generation and nation we see the mysterious confluence of human free will and the divine will of God guiding the course of human history.

God was sovereignly guiding the reign of King David just as much as the reign of King Nebuchadnezzar. God was just as sovereign in the leadership of David, who was called a man after God's own heart, as in that of David's son, King Solomon, who built the temple in Israel. God was just as sovereignly guiding the reign of King Nebuchadnezzar in Babylon, who destroyed that same temple.

For most of history, people had little or no say in who their leaders were. The human free will in question was not the outcome of democratic elections but the beliefs, actions, and character of the leader. Some were extraordinarily wise and led their people well through eras of prosperity and days of danger, conflict, and hardships alike. There were leaders who valued humility and honor and who carried the burden of their people's well-being close to heart. History is also filled with leaders who were prideful, arrogant, entitled, unjust, and malicious. There were leaders fueled by blind ambition, who thought little of what was best for the people under their authority.

In either case, the divine hand of God guiding the course of human events never faltered. Further, God provided wisdom and counsel to leaders throughout history. The most repeated verse in the Bible is some variation of the words, "God said to Moses." This phrase appears first in Exodus 6:10 and is repeated seventy-one times. The kings of Israel had access to the written law and words of the prophets. God sent Joseph to advise Pharaoh in Egypt and to manage the food supply to provide during years of famine and drought. God also sent Daniel, Shadrach, Meshach, and Abednego to advise King Nebuchadnezzar and govern over the affairs of Babylon.

God's sovereignty over the course of human history is best seen through the events recorded in the Book of Esther. Esther was queen of Persia and married to King Ahasuerus. In this story, we read of an insidious plot to exterminate the Jewish population living under the authority of the Persian Empire. It was a plot masterminded by a high-ranking official in the Persian court, Haman. Unknown to either Haman or King Ahasuerus, Queen Esther herself was Jewish. Her real name was Hadassah, and she was the orphaned cousin of the prophet Mordecai.

More than incidentally, the story of Esther is a gold mine of insights and advice for intentionally engaging leaders through prayer, respect, and humble submission to their authority. Esther is a story of faithful people fervently committing their leaders and potentially disastrous policies to God in prayer. Having done so, the people then trust that God will always work in the events of human history to save and deliver them. Mordecai sends word to Esther saying, "Don't think that you will escape the fate of all the Jews because you are in the king's palace. If you keep silent at this time, relief and deliverance will come to the Jewish people from another place, but you and your father's family will be destroyed." We then read perhaps the best-known statement from the entire book. The next words from Mordecai are a frequent source of encouragement to the elected leaders I know. Mordecai says, "Who knows, perhaps you have come to your royal position for such a time as this."[8]

For our present purposes, however, consider that God is never mentioned in the Book of Esther. Though undeniably the most important character in the story, the name of God does not appear in the text. Instead, the one writing the story draws our attention to the people who are threatened and the high-ranking officials making decisions. That is the natural way to write history. In our day, those writing the narrative of human events tend to focus on the leaders and particular players at the center of local, national, and world events. The lesson to be learned is that a higher power with ultimate authority is at work as well. We can be sure that the sovereign hand of God is guiding human history, even when the people in positions of power fail to mention it and may not even know God's name.

In modern times of democracy and representative government, the beliefs, actions, and character of the leader remain important to the factor of human free will. Now, the democratic process adds the beliefs, actions, and character of those who elect them. Increasing the power democratically held by the people does not infringe upon God's sovereignty. The primary difference is the degree to which we are all now accountable for the unfolding events of history. Your vote really does count, and the ability to choose leaders is both a blessing and great responsibility. Unfortunately, the human progress of democracy does not guarantee people will choose well. Nations elect leaders who are morally good just as they elect leaders who are morally flawed.

To say political leaders are chosen servants means greater responsibility for those who elect them, as well as greater humility when thinking about the people who are elected to lead. In Oklahoma and across the US, every member of our state legislatures brings unique experiences, skills, and perspectives. We must trust that God sovereignly worked in the lives of each one, whomever they are and whatever their particular beliefs about God may be. They are the specific individuals God appointed and allowed to serve at this time.

The Strategy Today

Focusing on specific places, people, and attitudes is an essential element to Paul's strategy. Applying the same three elements, we can be just as strategic in making a positive impact and influence in our day. When considering the *place,* begin closest to home. Start with local communities, schools, cities, counties or municipalities, and the state where you live. Resist the temptation to think of national politics and leaders. This process applies to leaders at all levels, but there is a strategic advantage to homing in on the place where you live and work. The ancient wisdom from the prophet Jeremiah is still true today: "But seek the welfare of the city where I have sent you . . . and pray to the Lord on its behalf, for in its welfare you will find your welfare."[9] Your impact intensifies as you focus on the people and the place closest to where you live and work.

Now turn your attention to the *people* serving in positions of authority, the leaders in business, education, faith communities, and the government. Some of these leaders are wonderful public servants who simply love their communities. They may not have particular ambitions to rise in their level of leadership or pursue higher office in their state or our nation. But some of these leaders do. What better opportunity will you have to create a positive impact in their life and future leadership than when they are serving in state and local office? Forge a positive relationship with them now and see how they might be better leaders in the future as the wheels of their political fortunes turn.

The author of Proverbs reminds us that society thrives or suffers based upon the state of its leaders: "When the righteous flourish, the people rejoice, but when the wicked rule, people groan."[10] When focusing upon the people elected to lead in modern representative democracies, this wisdom rightly guides us when considering how we will vote. It should equally compel us to never neglect the extraordinary opportunity to encourage leaders and genuinely desire good things in their lives.

Finally, apply the third element of Paul's strategy by adopting an *attitude* of thankfulness. Setting political agendas aside to genuinely express gratitude preserves your ability to meaningfully engage leaders, no matter who they are or whether you agree with them or not. Setting aside political agendas to pray for leaders with an attitude of thankfulness for their service and work can motivate leaders to govern better, work better, and be better. If you believe the

★ ★ ★ ★ ★

Bible as I do, then leaders are simply people we know God loves. The most significant way we can influence them for the long haul is to do so with absolute sincerity and with a genuine thankfulness for them, offering intercession on their behalf. When our leaders are better, we are all better. *Believe* leaders matter.

Chapter 4

★ ★ ★ ★ ★

When We Need a Different Perspective

The Perfect Way is only difficult for those who pick and choose . . . If you want the truth to stand clear before you, never be for or against. The struggle between "for" and "against" is the mind's worst disease.

—Sen-ts'an[1]

Our First Responsibility to Leaders

Believing leaders matter came as a direct result of my work to shape a positive leadership culture among Oklahoma policymakers. I based my approach on a first-century letter from the Apostle Paul to his friend and protégé Timothy, who was tasked with leading a Christian church started by Paul in the city of Ephesus:

First of all, then, I urge that petitions, prayers, intercessions, and thanksgivings be made for everyone, for kings and all those who are in authority, so that we may lead a tranquil and quiet life in all godliness and dignity. This is good, and it pleases God our Savior, who wants everyone to be saved and to come to the knowledge of the truth.[2]

Paul was not aware his letter would one day be included in Christian Scripture. His purpose was to instruct Timothy and the church in Ephesus to approach governmental leaders in a particular way that he believed would benefit the people in the church and the governmental leaders themselves, as well as the communities in and around Ephesus extending across the region.

Nearly two millennia later, this passage constitutes a biblical command to do three things:

1. Adopt an attitude of thanksgiving for leaders.

2. Intercede for leaders, desiring the best for them.

3. Do the first two without any political agenda.

For those who agree this is more than the advice of one leader to another but now carries the weight of a biblical command, are you faithfully praying for leaders in this way? I have a lot of conversations about this passage from 1 Timothy, and there seems to be a consensus: *Yes,* we have a clear biblical command to pray with thanksgiving and sincerity for our leaders, no matter who they are. *No,* we are not convinced we are being faithful to pray the way this scripture intends us to. That was certainly true of me, and, like everything else the Bible says about how to live, I am a work in progress. Some days are better than others, but I am getting better at putting these three principles of praying for leaders into practice.

On the other hand, perhaps you are not convinced this passage constitutes a biblical command. A lot has changed in government, and there are many differences between living in a first-century Roman colony and the United States in 2020. On face value, this is a letter from Paul to his friend Timothy, advising how best to approach the governing authorities in Ephesus. Even if this passage is nothing more than good advice, adopting an attitude of thanksgiving and desiring the best for leaders without any political agenda is wise and relevant counsel. Following the advice from Paul can open doors to productive dialogue with leaders, particularly when they are ones with whom you do not agree.

Whether a biblical command to pray or just good advice, adopting an attitude of thanksgiving and desiring the best for leaders without any political agenda is a starting point for breaking free of the incivility plaguing our politics. We need a change in perspective for the way we think of the political process, institutions, and the people in positions of leadership. With a new perspective, you discover an internal strength that cannot be defeated by whatever happens in our politics. That strength will bring confidence, peace, and the ability to think and respond to current and future events in more thoughtful and productive ways.

Four Shifts in Perspective

Let's look to the Apostle Paul to consider how we might change our perspective. His letter to Timothy gives insight into that transformed perspective. Taking the time to understand the context of the instruction to pray for leaders in 1 Timothy, we identify four distinct shifts that Paul has in mind, which will result in the needed change in perspective.

First, Paul challenges his readers to change their perspective of themselves. Second, he challenges their perspective of the nature of authority itself and where final authority resides. Third, Paul challenges their perspective of leaders. Fourth, Paul challenges his reader to take up the specific tactic of praying for leaders.

Look again at the first two verses: "First of all, then, I urge that supplications, prayers, intercessions, and thanksgivings be made for all people, for kings and all who are in high positions." Imagine Paul is writing directly to you and you heed his instruction to pray. Even if offered in private, there are at least three participants involved in such a prayer: the person praying (you), the higher authority prayed to (God), and the person (political leader) for whom you pray. How you view each of these three participants shapes how you feel about politics and political leaders, as well as how you engage in the political process. Your perspective on each of these participants can determine whether you will break through the incivility or perpetuate it.

Look back at 1 Timothy 2:1-2 and notice the presence of the word *then* or *therefore* at the beginning of verse 1. This word indicates context. Paul's instruction to pray for leaders in this way is based on something he already said. We need to look at the preceding verses to understand what that is. Backing up three verses to read, we find the following: "This charge I entrust to you, Timothy, my child, in accordance with the prophecies previously made about you, that by them you may wage the good warfare."[3]

Is this approach simply my way of telling you to calm down and stop caring so much about what happens in our country, cities, and states? To borrow another often used phrase of Paul, by no means! Christians do not sit back and wait for the world to pass us by. To the contrary, Paul wants his reader to wage the good warfare. This call to action is reminiscent of Shakespeare's King Henry V, when stirring the courage of his army who were vastly outnumbered to believe victory was possible. "We few, we happy few," the warrior poet and king cries, "we band of brothers; for he today that sheds his blood with me shall be my brother."[4]

Like Shakespeare's warrior king, Paul rallies the courage to act but also warns the reader to "have faith and a good conscience. Some have rejected these and have shipwrecked their faith."[5] He then refers to two examples, Hymenaeus and Alexander. We do not know the precise circumstances of their story or why Paul brings them up, but Timothy probably did. They were people Timothy knew and likely worked with. Ultimately, Paul mentions Hymenaeus and Alexander because they were two individuals who shipwrecked their faith by rejecting something. What did they reject?

One thing they rejected was a good conscience. Simply put, the conscience is the rudder that guides your life and ultimately your thoughts and behavior. Carefully consider the promptings of your conscience and beware when negative and resentful thoughts influence your attitude. The way we think shapes the attitude of our hearts. The words we say and the things we do naturally follow. This is why the author of Ecclesiastes teaches that God will judge every deed and every hidden thought.[6]

The Bible teaches that the Christian's conscience is informed and indwelt by the Holy Spirit, who nudges their heart to consider whether what they are doing or even thinking about may be wrong. The conscience tells us that what we are thinking or dwelling upon is more self-centered than Christ-centered, focused on ourselves more than others. This is happening all the time. We are constantly veering left and right of Christ-centeredness. The Holy Spirit-informed conscience within you is the rudder continually righting the course.

According to Paul, Hymenaeus and Alexander either ignored the pull of the rudder against their hearts or they ripped the steering wheel out altogether and tossed it overboard. You can only ignore your conscience for so long. We don't know the precise details of Hymenaeus's and Alexander's story, but Timothy likely did. Whether by continuously fighting their conscience or ignoring it altogether, the result is the same: a rudderless ship drifting until meeting destruction. The Christian life is not to be this way.

Hymenaeus and Alexander did not only reject their conscience. Keeping with Paul's metaphor of sailing a ship, there also exists a single point of reference. It was often a point of light in the sky, such as the North Star, that guides the way. Just as a skilled navigator does not abandon his guiding lodestar, the Christian must keep in their sights a primary objective. To the Philippian church, Paul called it the *faith of the gospel*,[7] and in this letter to Timothy, Paul simply calls it *the faith*. What is *the faith* exactly? Back up a few more verses to see how Paul describes it:

> I give thanks to Christ Jesus our Lord who has strengthened me, because he considered me faithful, appointing me to the ministry—even though I was formerly a blasphemer, a persecutor, and an arrogant man. But I received mercy because I acted out of ignorance in unbelief, and the grace of our Lord overflowed, along with the faith and love that are in Christ Jesus.[8]

Don't miss the all-important phrase in verse 14: "I acted out of ignorance in unbelief." Paul is not excusing or absolving himself in any way. He was an idolatrous, brutal, murderous, and violent hater of other people. He was guilty. But notice, there is an understanding that those who do not share his Christian faith are acting out of some level of ignorance. This is certainly true, for how can anyone fully understand the perspective and motivations of Paul if he has not received the same mercy in his heart? Mercy would be enough, but in Paul's words from verse 14, both mercy "and the grace of our Lord overflowed, along with the faith and love that are in Christ Jesus."

Reflect on your own life for a moment. What is your story? From what did Jesus rescue you? Where were you before you experienced the mercy, grace, love, and forgiveness found at the foot of the cross? No matter where you were or what you had done, you were forgiven, washed clean, and made whole. Paul is not using the word *ignorance* in a pejorative, condescending, or inflammatory sense. He simply means that anyone who has not experienced such mercy, grace, and faith does not know or understand why Christians believe as they do in God, Jesus, the Bible, and the church.

In verse 15, Paul writes what he really means by *the faith*: "The saying is trustworthy and deserving of full acceptance, Christ Jesus came into the world to save sinners, of whom I am the foremost."[9] In this letter, Paul reminds Timothy that the Christian faith has a primary mission and purpose that motivates every endeavor: Jesus Christ came to save sinners.

There is nothing new or surprising in Paul's definition of *the faith* found here in 1 Timothy. An introductory knowledge of Christian teaching typically includes the idea that Jesus saves sinners. The phrase "Jesus saves" can be cliché or good fodder for dry doctrinal statements of faith incorporated into the bylaws of a church. On the other hand, there are those who believe this is true with every fiber of their being. They believe in a magnificent and Holy God. Having never committed half of the horrible things Paul did, such people nod their heads when reading the phrase, "Christ Jesus came into the world to save sinners, of whom I am foremost," knowing how hopelessly broken and sinful they were. The message that Jesus saves is no cliché; rather, it is the only way to approach a Holy God. For people who believe the faith of the gospel as Paul did, Jesus Christ coming to earth to stand in their place and receive the penalty for their sin is a message of life, hope, and lasting peace.

Paul continues writing that those who share this faith have a responsibility to do something with it, writing in verse 16, "But I received mercy for this reason, that in me, as the foremost, Jesus Christ might display his perfect patience as an example to those who were to believe in him for eternal life." I praise God that it is Jesus' patience and not mine that matters. There is no one whose sin is so egregious that they are beyond Jesus' patience to forgive. There is no nation so twisted or lost that the transforming power of the gospel cannot redeem it.

However, Paul taught this message of the faith includes a hard truth that can be difficult to hear. The sin that separates a person from God has also turned their passions against God. People are not just apart from God but opposed to God. Read how the English

Standard Version translates 1 Timothy 1:13: "Though formerly I was a blasphemer, persecutor, and insolent opponent." Paul viewed himself as an insolent opponent, not merely of Christians but of God. In the account of Paul's conversion recorded in Acts 9:4, Jesus says to Paul, "'Saul, Saul, why are you persecuting me?'" The great tragedy of our world is how many people do not know their sin not only separates them but also sets their lives against God. Paul would say that they, ignorant in their unbelief, have both rejected and opposed their own creator.

How does God respond to this opposition? The Bible consistently says that God responds with love, patience, and a longing to forgive sin. In Numbers 14:18, we read, "The Lord is slow to anger and abounding in faithful love, forgiving iniquity and rebellion." The psalmist writes in Psalm 86:15, "But you, Lord, are a compassionate and gracious God, slow to anger and abounding in faithful love and truth." The Apostle Peter writes in 2 Peter 3:9, "The Lord does not delay his promise, as some understand delay, but is patient with you, not wanting any to perish but all to come to repentance." Paul writes in Romans 5:8, "But God proves his own love for us in that while we were still sinners, Christ died for us."

We learn from Paul, through this definition of the faith, that there are many things churches *can do* and many things they *will do*. There are just as many things churches will not do that they *should do*. Christians believe that all people are sinners, and because of love for every last one, Jesus Christ came to save sinners. Set before us as a fixed point of light in the sky that guides us, there is the one absolute and non-negotiable thing that we *must do*. Christians must share this message of mercy, grace, and love. It is a simple message that there is peace at the cross of Jesus Christ. It is a message of peace that is for all people.

Why am I telling you this? I am not trying to sound preachy or slip in an evangelistic message. Instead, consider how this understanding of *the faith* forever changed Paul's life. Most important, this message changed the way he saw himself. Immediately following the words "Jesus Christ came into the world to save sinners," Paul writes, "of whom I am the foremost."

Shift One: How You View Yourself

Paul once saw the world as comprised of different kinds of people who belonged to different categories. Some people were Roman citizens, and others were not. He also saw some people as Jews while others were Gentiles. Within Judaism, there were those who faithfully kept the Law of Moses and followed the teachings of the Prophets, and there were those he believed did not, such as these new followers of Jesus. But all these divisions fade after hearing and believing the simple message of peace through the faith in Jesus.

Here is the first perspective change for Paul: *he no longer viewed the world in terms of us and them but in terms of we and Him.* Paul learned to see all people as equal and, equally, as sinners. The only division that ultimately mattered to him was the one separating God and humanity.

When we think in terms of us and them, we attach value to various groups and usually think one is good and the other is bad. We typically see whatever group we are in as right and the others as wrong. Many times, we justify our group as being on God's side. When we think in terms of we and Him, however, we understand that no one was on God's side. All people had turned their backs on God and rejected His lordship.

When we think in terms of us and them, we will inevitably begin thinking in terms of us versus them. Doing this means all the man-made things that divide us can become unholy hills upon which we fight bitterly against one another. But when we think in terms of we and Him, we will cross oceans and traverse cultures to become part of them because the Lamb of God died on the darkest of unholy hills bearing the wrath of God poured out on the sin of the world.

Continue thinking in terms of us and them, and we will become more stratified and bitterly disdainful of one another, fearful of one another. Begin thinking in terms of we and Him and begin proclaiming greater is the one thing that unites all humanity but divides us from God. The only divide that matters is the divide of sin that is common to all of us.

Those who think in terms of we and Him see beyond every man-made division: race, religion, gender, and nationality. We are all one, creatures of God's handiwork and imprinted with the image of God. With this shift in perspective, we commit to seeing the world no longer in terms of us and them but we and Him. Are you opposed to Him or reconciled to Him?

Shift Two: How You View God

The gospel message can be a difficult challenge to people blessed to live as citizens of strong and free nations such as America. It is far too easy to trust in the strength of a strong country. In 2017, James Mattis spoke to John Dickerson on CBS's *Face the Nation*. Dickerson asked the newly minted US Secretary of Defense what threats around the world kept him awake at night. He responded, in true Mattis form, "Nothing. I keep others awake at night." Mattis did not diminish the threats to national security and the world, but his response reminded the interviewer and all who watched that the United States' military and defense apparatus was the most powerful and capable fighting force in the world.[10]

The same was true of the Roman Empire in the first century. There was no more skilled, dangerous, and overwhelming power than the legions of soldiers serving Cesar. However, when Paul wanted his readers to see nation-states, governments, and armies—

in all their power and might—as things that will not last. Read on to verse 17: "No we do not trust in nations—but to the King of the Ages, immortal, invisible, the only God, be honor and glory forever and ever. Amen."

If the powerful and enduring Roman Empire did not last, what will? Speaking to the people of Athens, Acts 17:26 records Paul saying of God, "From one man he has made every nationality to live over the whole earth and has determined their appointed times and the boundaries of where they live." God alone is the eternal, immortal, ultimate power and source of all authority. Think of the words in Psalm 46:6: "Nations rage, kingdoms topple; the earth melts when he lifts his voice."[11]

Whatever institution, government, or authority appears dominant on the world stage, Paul views God as the only king of every age past, present, and in the future. Seeing God this way leads to the second shift in Paul's perspective: *no longer trusting in earthly institutions, nations, and people but trusting in a higher authority*. For Paul, that higher authority is God, the King of Kings and Lord of an eternal kingdom.

When we place our trust in a higher authority than institutions, government, or people in positions of authority, the divisions, debates, and conflicts that consume our political discourse evaporate. Now, all we see are people living at a particular point in human history and under the authority of God. Some people live in relative comfort and security while others are afraid, angry, or in need. Jesus claimed He possessed all authority in one of the last things He said to His disciples while on earth: "All authority has been given to me in heaven and on earth. Go, therefore, and make disciples of all nations . . . teaching them to observe everything I have commanded in. And remember, I am with you always."[12] All people need to know Jesus Christ came to save sinners.

Why am I telling you this? I do not diminish the significance of governments or the importance of the policies they debate. This whole passage in 1 Timothy culminates with a biblical command to pray for them because they matter and are appointed by God. But we must pray with a better perspective on those governments and policies. If you believe as Paul did, then you know all governments are temporary and there is another kingdom that existed for millennia before now and will exist for all eternity after this one. Paul believed that God's sovereign reign over the affairs of humanity has been and will always be found true.

Shift Three: How You View Leaders

Paul invites his reader to view themselves as a forgiven member of one human race living under the authority of one eternal God. In 1 Timothy 1:18, he now commissions his reader to wage the good warfare of the faith and draws their attention to a strategic place to begin: with *leaders*.

But we must understand a king, or any person in authority, as Timothy—as well as the people he led in Ephesus—would understand them. Governments have progressed a great deal since the days of the Roman Empire when this letter was first written. They've introduced democracy, the rule of law, and human rights. People now look to government and public policies for a multitude of purposes and functions, such as social services, healthcare, education, public safety, military defense, scientific research, and the list goes on.

Governments in the first century served multiple functions as well, but their primary purpose was keeping a peaceful and orderly society. Keeping peace and order were undeniably in the domain of government. Neither Jesus, Paul, nor any of the early church leaders sought to change that. Across his writings, Paul was consistent in this view of the role of government. To the church in Rome, he clearly states that governments are God's appointed instruments to maintain order:

Let everyone submit to the governing authorities, since there is no authority except from God, and the authorities that exist are instituted by God . . . For it is God's servant for your good. But if you do wrong, be afraid, because it does not carry the sword for no reason. For it is God's servant, an avenger that brings wrath on the one who does wrong.[13]

According to Paul's instruction in 1 Timothy 2, we should be thankful for those in governmental authority fulfilling their duty to maintain order. Many churches place special emphasis around key dates that honor the people who lead in government, especially those who serve in uniform to promote freedom and safety in our country as well as around the world. Calling our hearts to be thankful for those who serve to maintain order and fight for a more peaceful, free, and dignified world is appropriate.

However, notice the intended result of this prayer found in 1 Timothy 2:2: "That we may lead a peaceful and quiet life, godly and dignified in every way." The intended result of this prayer is a peaceful and quiet life. This means that Paul's instruction on prayer shares a warning. Beware what underlying motivations guide the way you pray for governmental and political leaders and set them aside. If our aim is to be faithful to this text, then no matter how selfless or sincere our intentions or opinions may be and no matter how good or God-honoring they may be, we need to set aside all political motivations and agenda when we pray for our leaders.

Here is why. Our desire may be for our leaders to make decisions and choices that honor God and benefit others. We may long for the gospel to redeem our country and our culture, and we may believe the decisions that are made by our leaders can promote or hinder this noble goal. After all, keep reading verses 3 and 4 of 1 Timothy 2: "This is good, and it pleases God our Savior, who wants everyone to be saved and to come to the knowledge of the truth." So how can these motivations be wrong?

The noblest of intentions can be wrong when we fail to recognize the limits of our knowledge and wisdom. The Book of Proverbs goes to great lengths to teach us that no one person has all the answers. Even the very best of us sees only partly what is good, true, and right. We need the perspective, experience, and wisdom of others. Further, human beings have a tendency toward selfishness and often fail to recognize their own bias. Consider the ancient wisdom found in Proverbs 21:2: "All a person's ways seem right to him, but the LORD weighs hearts." I need the humility to say that I do not know what direction and path is ultimately the best because I do not weigh the hearts of people. Only God does that.

I also need the discipline and wisdom to engage with people holding views different than my own. James 3:17 says, "The wisdom from above is first pure, then peace-loving, gentle, compliant, full of mercy and good fruits, unwavering, without pretense." Warren Wiersbe describes *compliant* as willing to hear all sides without compromising your own convictions.[14] Political discourse could stand to have more of this sort of wisdom, to hear another person's point of view with a willingness to be convinced.

We, ourselves, need the humility to recognize our own limits and the wisdom to learn from others, but we also need these traits in our leaders. This is why Paul tells Timothy to focus on leaders, for we can pray for every person in a position of authority to gain such humility and wisdom. This leads to the third shift in perspective: *view leaders as people and separate from the particular leadership position they hold*. The person is not the same thing as their position, and we can hold the two in distinction to focus on them as *people*.

Leaders quickly become exaggerations of themselves based on our prejudices and personal opinions of the politics, party, policies, or principles they seem to represent. Thinking of leaders this way leads us down destructive paths identified by many leadership authors, paths of *hero-worship* as well as *scapegoating*.[15] Our opinions of them become formed by whether or not their politics align with our own. Thinking too highly of a leader you agree with can set you up to be disappointed by them and disillusioned altogether. Alternatively, demonizing and dehumanizing leaders when we disagree with their principles or position reduces them to less than a person, which is the worst thing anyone can ever do to someone else.

Begin to think of leaders as people just like anyone else. Any impulse within you to disrespect another person should be reason enough to give you pause. Regarding the words we say, James writes, "With [our tongues] we bless our Lord and Father, and with it we curse people who are made in the likeness of God . . . these things ought not to be so."[16] Every person is made in the likeness of God, having inherent dignity and being worthy of respect and kindness.

Leaders can lose our respect. Paul writes in Romans 13:7, "Pay to all what is owed to them: taxes to whom taxes are owed, revenue to whom revenue is owed, respect to whom respect is owed, honor to whom honor is owed" (ESV). There are certainly instances where the behavior and actions of leaders appropriately lead to a loss of respect where they no longer deserve to be honored. Far too often, however, we refuse to show the initial respect and honor that all people deserve—typically solely on the basis of someone's politics. We take personal offense to their politics and perpetuate a cycle of incivility.

Learning to distinguish between the person and their position allows you to remain objective and become less likely to fall prey to the toxic outrage and hostility surrounding politics. Heifetz writes, "Distinguishing [position] from [person] is not a prescription for keeping emotions—values and passions—at a distance . . . But it enables [you] not to be misled by [your] emotions into taking statements and events personally that might have little to do with [you]."[17]

Finally, remember that in a representative democracy our leaders are elected to speak for the needs and principles shared by the people they represent. Thinking of each leader as a person reminds us that they are one of many people from the communities they represent. Elected leaders come from different places and represent diverse populations. The priorities, principles, and policies of one legislative district may not be the same as those of another. There are times when the needs of one community inform and align with the needs of others. There are also times when the interests of different communities conflict with the interests of others, and we shouldn't be offended or surprised when they do. We need people who can skillfully and respectfully navigate those areas of conflict and disagreement. That is a time when leaders especially matter.

Shift Four: Choosing the Tactics of Prayer

With new perspective on yourself, God, and leaders, accept Paul's challenge to consider your choice of tactics. This is the fourth shift in perspective and what the instruction in 1 Timothy 2:1-2 is really all about: *do not look to the tactics of politics but look first to the tactics of prayer.*

Participating in the political process and advocacy can take on many forms. There can be well-organized letter writing campaigns or efforts to mobilize constituents to speak to their legislator. Public demonstrations, rallies, and protests have grown in popularity and frequency in recent years. Others will choose to donate to political campaigns, volunteer, or run for office themselves. Of course, the ability to vote is an extraordinary blessing that hasn't existed for much of human history and is not the political reality for everyone today. All of these forms of participation can be effective and appropriate forms of political engagement at times and under various circumstances.

As effective as these tactics are, Paul writes that there is a greater power and resource available to us, one more effective than anything else. Those who share Paul's new perspective of themselves, the nature of authority, and leaders do not trust in strength or might, in people or nations, in economics or politics. Rather, they trust in greatest resource and power on earth imaginable: *prayer.* It is available at any moment and anywhere on earth. We can pray for our leaders, whoever and wherever they are and at any point of the day. Paul longed for his readers to take hold of the power of prayer and begin by praying for their leaders.

When trying to sincerely pray for leaders and those in authority, policy outcomes and political agendas get in the way. There can be a natural inclination to pray for a specific decision, outcome, or direction. We want to pray for leaders to do what we want them to do—or not do. Paul wisely instructs his reader to focus on the leaders themselves and not the particular policies or actions we may want from them.

Allowing specific bills or legislation to consume our focus unnecessarily limits our view of the responsibilities and decisions we expect of political leaders. A person's time in office encompasses numerous bills addressing a range of policy issues and sectors of society. Additionally, concentrating on specific legislation is not helpful because we don't always know what it is we are praying for. The path we will take, plan we should follow, or the policy that finally will be implemented is rarely known or even clear to us. It is often in the very last hour that the final details of public policy come together.

On the other hand, the people in the positions of leadership who negotiate and craft those policies are known to us by name.

We can pray for God to heal and restore broken lives and systems throughout our nation, states, cities, and neighborhoods. Paul's instruction on prayer does not ignore the significant impact of governmental leaders and policies. Rather, Paul teaches us to pray for God to first bless the hearts and lives of our leaders. Pray for each one to have wisdom and the endurance to lead with grace and integrity in all the decisions they must make throughout their term. Pray for the people and with no other agenda whatsoever.

The message of the gospel also transformed the way Paul understood the power of prayer. When Paul was in prison in Rome and writing to the church in Philippi, he genuinely believed he could die that day. Yet Paul was convinced that everything would work out for his deliverance *through* the prayers of the church. Paul believed prayer would change his situation.

Throughout the Bible, we see this same belief in the power of prayer. The power of prayer is mysterious. I do not know why God made prayer to work this way, and I do not completely understand how it works. Regardless, in God's divine design, He has made it such that the praying of His people changes things. Paul's instruction to Timothy leaves us with two questions to answer: What do we pray for? Who do we pray for?

Who do we pray for? We pray for leaders and all those in authority because the power they steward will affect many people and can create the best possible environment for more people to live and thrive.

What do we pray for? We pray for the gospel to advance, first in the hearts of our leaders and then in their heads. We pray for them to have humility and wisdom as they speak to one another and work together. We pray for the people serving in positions of authority so that the policies they implement might create the best possible opportunity for peace and prosperity to advance in our neighborhoods, churches, and schools. And we pray for leaders so that the decisions they make will cause all in our cities, states, and nation and the world to thrive.

One Final Observation

Here is one last observation from this passage in 1 Timothy. Before singling out the rulers and those in authority, Paul instructs Timothy to pray for all people because God desires all people to be saved and come to the knowledge of the truth. By telling Timothy to pray for all people, however, Paul is not giving an excuse for us to be lazy in our praying. We are not to pray like this: "Thank you, God, for my family, for my health, my home, and my job. God, I just want to thank you for all the ways you bless me and so many people. God, I pray for all people. I know you love everyone, so I pray for you to take care of all people. Amen."

Paul wants his reader to understand that prayer is the most powerful spiritual resource imaginable. As such, he is not giving license to pray broad prayers, but he is enlisting us to pray bold prayers. If you believe in the faith of the gospel as Paul did, then there is no one you can't pray for, so I urge you to pray for all people and to begin with your leaders.

If you believe as Paul did, then you are forgiven. So, pray and give thanks to God because, first and foremost, Jesus Christ came to save sinners, and by His blood, He has made you righteous. Leaders have personal faults and failures just as we all do, so pray for them to experience forgiveness in their own lives. If you believe as Paul did, then do not misplace your trust in the institutions of this world but pray to the great King of Ages, who is the immortal, invisible, and only wise God. There is a higher authority than the institutions and governments that appear so great in the world today. Pray for leaders to work wisely and do as much good as they can while in office. But remember that every leader serves only for a moment in time. New laws will be written, and there will be others who come after them.

If you believe as Paul did, then do not sit idly by as world events tick across your television, laptop, or social media feed. You are called to engage in the world around you. Pray for leaders to champion their personal convictions and represent the needs of their respective districts to the very best of their ability. If you believe as Paul did, then do not resort to the tactics of politics but first take up the most powerful weapon the world has ever known and pray bold prayers. Pray for the people elected to your state legislature and pray for your governor. Pray for the mayor, police officers, and first responders. Pray for our president, members of Congress, and for the leaders of foreign nations.

Lastly, if you believe as Paul did, then do not give in to the culture of incivility and hostility rampant in political discourse today. Resist the forces in culture seeking to divide society into endless affinity groups that oppose one another. Think of leaders first of all as people and more than whatever position of authority they currently hold. Take up the tactics of prayer because the Bible promises that God hears us when we pray. Remember another promise from the Bible: "The prayer of a righteous person has great power as it is working."[18]

If you do not believe in the message of the gospel as Paul did, the four shifts in perspective still remain a relevant and useful framework for engaging leaders and breaking through the incivility in our politics. First, resist looking at culture in terms of us and them, which breaks down society into divisions and factions. Second, remember that institutional and governmental authority is not ultimate. The United States is a constitutional democracy granting limited power that is ultimately derived from the people. Third, separate the people from their respective positions of authority and thereby restore a basic sense of respect and decency when interacting with leaders. Finally, choose better tactics for engaging with leaders and participating in the political process. Chapter 5 will consider alternative approaches if prayer is not your normal practice.

Ask More *for* Leaders

*[Prayer] is the most dynamic work which God
has entrusted to His saints, but it is also the
most neglected ministry open to the believer.*

—D. Edmond Hiebert[1]

*Prayer is an indispensable part of the Christian's life
and of the church's life. And the church's first duty
toward society and its leaders is to pray for them.*

—John Stott[2]

*And this is the confidence that we have toward him,
that if we ask anything according to his will he hears us.*

—1 John 5:14

Chapter 5

★ ★ ★ ★ ★

Through Prayer

Prayer does not prepare us for the greater work.
Prayer is the greater work.

—Oswald Chambers[1]

A Sacred Moment

I have worked for a number of years as a chaplain in the Oklahoma State Capitol. One of my primary responsibilities is to open official events and legislative sessions in prayer. When doing so, I stand at a podium in the well of that ornate legislative chamber. In front of me are elected representatives and senators, and we are surrounded by an upper gallery that is filled with visitors to the Capitol, legislative staff, and all the people working to craft public policy.

The prayer lasts no more than a few minutes before a full day with its packed agenda begins. It can easily be considered as a relatively minor item in the overall scheme of things. Brief as it is, offering this opening prayer is a great privilege and no small thing. I never want to find myself thinking that something small cannot be profound.

I view those first few moments as sacred—and for good reason. I'm not naïve, and none of us should fool ourselves. We ought to know that the members of these legislative bodies are not always in agreement. In fact, there is a wide spectrum of opinion and varied levels of agreement and disagreement on a host of issues and policies.

In Oklahoma, we have 101 members of the House of Representatives and forty-eight members of the Senate. They come from all across the state and represent diverse communities with diverse constituencies. Each district represented has very real but very different needs and challenges, as well as resources, they bring to the Capitol. Each district is represented by elected leaders who are just as diverse. They have different backgrounds and education and unique life experiences, and they work in different industries and sectors. Each one has important skills and needed perspective.

We do not send them to the Capitol because they already agree with each other but to discuss and debate the policies that affect all of us. We do expect them to reason together and navigate those areas of disagreement. We do not want them to abandon their principles but to bring their principles into fruitful dialogue with the positions and priorities of others. Ultimately, we send them to do the hard work, as best they are able, and craft public policy that charts a path forward for all in our state.

The opening prayer is called an invocation, and I realize the time is very short. Brief though it may be, it is a sacred moment to invoke God's blessing on each of them before their work begins, a moment spent in quiet prayer and a moment that humbles everyone in the room and places them side-by-side as equals. For those members in the chamber, it is a moment to ask God to bless someone you are preparing to debate. That moment can elevate the tone with which our leaders engage each other. I've seen it happen. This brief moment spent in prayer also contains the potential to elevate the substance of the debate itself. What we really want in complicated policy debates are better ideas that lead to better solutions. Yes, it is a sacred moment.

Prayer as Communication

If the second step of this process is to ask more *for* leaders, prayer is an obvious way to do that. As a chaplain, it is obvious that I would choose prayer as a method. Ultimately, prayer is a form of communication. That is true whether you are a person who regularly prays, occasionally prays, or rarely or never does. As communication, prayer becomes a conversation that is immensely beneficial. It can be an internal dialogue primarily for personal benefit or a chance to process and think through various ideas, feelings, and potential actions as they play out in conversational form. Prayer can be a form of conversation between people where they listen better to the thoughts and desires of one another. Most commonly, prayer is thought of as a conversation between a person and God. It is an appeal to a higher authority or divine power.

Whatever your personal experience and practice, when contemplating prayer for leaders and those in positions of authority, there may be a few questions forming in your mind right now: Why should I pray? How should I pray? What if I don't pray? If I do, what should I pray?

Why Should I Pray for Leaders?

Let's address these questions for both people who do pray and for those who may not. In both instances, answers to these questions flow from the distinctive elements in the prayer for governmental leaders from 1 Timothy 2:1-4. Remember from this passage that Paul instructs his readers to pray "for kings and all those who are in authority."[2] In our day, we understand "kings and all those who are in authority" as political and governmental leaders. That list does not stop at the president of the United States and the top leaders in Washington. "All those in authority" applies to state and local leaders, judges, law enforcement officers, school principals, and more.

Remember, too, this passage tells us to pray with thanksgiving, making intercession for leaders. That's very hard to do when you don't know who your leaders are, and it's almost impossible when you don't agree with your leaders or didn't vote for them. The kings and ruling authorities at the time 1 Timothy was written were certainly people with whom Paul's readers would not agree. Even still, the command to pray for them with gratitude and make intercession is clearly stated. The Bible also refers to governmental leaders as God's servants.[3]

Now, the government is not the same thing as the church, but the Bible calls governmental leaders God's servants, nonetheless. They are the people appointed to serve at this particular time, whether you voted for them or not and whether you agree with them or not. In a representative democracy, we are blessed with a number of individuals who step out from their community to work on our behalf. Most important, these leaders are chosen by the people they represent. They come from diverse districts with different needs and challenges but also have resources to bring to the table. These are the people for whom we can ask for a growing sense of integrity, as well as for grace, wise counsel, encouragement, and support.

How Should I Pray for Leaders?

There are three distinct elements found in the 1 Timothy 2:1-4 prayer. If we wish to pray in the way this passage intends, there are three things we must do.

Adopt an attitude of thanksgiving. Remember that this prayer provides an opportunity to express gratitude and adopt a genuine attitude of thanksgiving for leaders. As I read the Bible, a clear pattern appears for how people are designed to live. Fully thriving as a person is linked to being thankful. This is seen throughout the Bible and exemplified across history in most every culture. Being thankful is indicative of the health and well-being of an individual and is also a mark of a thriving community of people. It is a good practice each year for families and friends to gather together and reflect on the many things for which they are thankful.

Prayer marked by thanksgiving also helps to calm anxiety and worry. Paul writes in Philippians 4:6-7, "Don't worry about anything, but in everything, through prayer and petition with thanksgiving, present your requests to God. And the peace of God, which surpasses all understanding, will guard your hearts and minds in Christ Jesus." Given the state of our political discourse, any practice that calms fears and anxiety is worth considering.

Make intercessions for leaders. The second distinction in the 1 Timothy prayer is to make intercessions for leaders. Intercession is a form of prayer that indicates the person being prayed for isn't actively part of the practice of prayer itself. To intercede on another person's behalf is to seek blessings, peace, and joy in their life. It doesn't matter if you know specific ways to pray. To intercede is to earnestly desire that the life of the person you are praying for is blessed.

The opportunity to talk with an elected leader's spouse or family is a great privilege when serving as a legislative chaplain. From them I get a behind-the-scenes look at how elected leaders carry the weight of their responsibilities:

> *I'm always praying for his health during the legislative session. One year he worked through the flu, two sinus infections, and pneumonia.*

> *She is always discouraged when having to turn down an invitation to attend an event in the district . . . She cannot be at everything, and our kids are still young.*

> *He just can't sleep, especially during legislative deadline week when he is concerned about keeping certain bills that will benefit our community alive during the session.*

> *One year, we had multiple deaths in our family, and she didn't have the chance to grieve. That was a very hard year.*

So many people are relying on him. He doesn't want to let them down.

Our family business normally doesn't require a lot of his attention during session, but we lost two major customers the same month![4]

These conversations have much to teach us about making intercession for our leaders. Life doesn't stop for elected leaders when they are at the Capitol. Interceding for them means we must pray for every aspect of their lives: Pray for their health. Pray for needed sleep. Pray for their marriages, children, and grandchildren. Pray for the responsibilities they still have outside of their task as legislators. Interceding means praying for these things and sincerely desiring the best for their life.

Have no agenda other than to bless leaders. Notice the third important distinction Paul makes in 1 Timothy. What was the intended result of this prayer? Was it to promote a specific policy? No. We keep reading and find the result: "So that we may lead a tranquil and quiet life in all godliness and dignity."[5] There is no policy or political agenda mentioned. The outcome of the prayer is that both the leader being prayed for and the person who prays will be blessed and at peace.

Paul goes on to write that praying for leaders is good and pleases God, our Savior, who desires all people to be saved and come to the knowledge of the truth. The outcome of our prayer should not be for a particular policy or political position to be achieved. The intended result is essentially to promote individual liberty and a mutual benefit between the authorities and the people who pray for them.

There is also a more practical reason we should choose to pray for the people and not specific policies. When specific policies or legislative bills become our focus, we don't really know what it is we are praying for. Very rarely are the final details of various policies known to us. Further, even what seems like good public policy can have unintended consequences. What we do know is this: the people who are doing that work and writing those policies are known to us by name. Pray for the people and not the policies.

What If I Don't Pray?

Participating in this step of the process is possible for someone who is not a person of prayer. In his book *Love Your Enemies: How Decent People Can Save America from the Culture of Contempt*, Arthur Brooks wades deep into this same discussion for how we can resolve the incivility that grips culture. As his subtitle suggests, Brooks identifies *contempt* as a prime culprit for the state of things and offers advice and strategies for defeating it. Brooks writes, "Gratitude is, quite simply, a contempt killer. You cannot have contempt for someone to whom you are grateful."[6]

To develop a strategy for cultivating gratitude, Brooks consulted a host of authorities, ranging from social scientists, neurological researchers, ancient philosophy, and biblical references. Anyone sincerely interested in how our culture can navigate away from of the incivility and vitriol gripping the culture (the sort of person likely reading this book) needs to get a copy of *Love Your Enemies* by Arthur Brooks.

Brooks also consulted a personal friend: His Holiness the Dalai Lama. He asked the spiritual leader of the Tibetan Buddhist people what to do when feeling contempt. Brooks was told he needed to, "practice warm-heartedness."[7] Brooks explains his reaction:

[At first I thought] it sounded more like an aphorism than useful counsel. But when I thought about it, I saw it was actually tough and practical advice. He was not advocating surrender to the views of those with whom we disagree. If I believe I am right, I have a duty to stick to my views. But my duty is also to be kind, fair, and friendly to all, even those with whom I have great differences . . . He told me: Think back to a time in your life when you answered contempt with warm-heartedness. Remember how it made you feel, and then do it again.[8]

Brooks concludes, "Kindness and warm-heartedness are the antivenom for the poisonous contempt coursing through the veins of our political discourse."[9] The most significant reason kindness and warm-heartedness effectively inoculate against contempt is how they remind us of the inherent dignity and worth of those with whom we disagree. Our political opponents are more than the condensed caricature of their particular position or party affiliation. Instead, kindness and warm-heartedness cause you to look at someone with whom you disagree *as a person* worthy of the same kindness and respect as any other. A path out from incivility and the culture of contempt is possible when we reclaim respect for the dignity and worth of every person in our society. For some, the way forward is kindness and warm-heartedness. For others, it can be through adopting an attitude of thanksgiving and intercession through prayer.

What Does Prayer Really Do?

For those who do pray, there are three additional encouragements about prayer we can learn from Paul's first letter to Timothy: prayer is powerful, pleases God, and reminds us where true power and authority reside.

Prayer is powerful. The verses just before the instruction to pray for leaders in 1 Timothy 2:1-4 remind us that God sent Jesus to the world to save sinners and no one is beyond the saving power of the gospel. As his followers, Paul then writes, we are to join in this one great mission of sharing the good news of the power of God through Christ. The four verses about prayer for governmental leaders serve, really, to tell us where to begin. For the cause of Christ who saves, we do not trust in strength or might, in people or nations, in economics or politics. Rather, we trust in the greatest resource and power on earth imaginable: *prayer*. It is available to us at any moment, anywhere on earth. We can pray for our leaders, no matter who they are, no matter where we are, and at any point of the day. Paul longed for the people of God to take hold of the power of prayer and to begin by praying for our leaders.

Prayer pleases God. The New International Version translates Proverbs 21:1 as, "In the Lord's hand the king's heart is a stream of water that he channels toward all who please him." The call to pray for leaders is a call for Christians to rediscover that power of prayer. It is a call to pray in a more biblical way by giving thanks and making intercession for leaders because that is a prayer and an attitude that pleases God.

Prayer reminds us where true authority resides. Before instructing the church to pray for leaders, Paul writes that Christians should give all glory and honor to the King of the Ages, the immortal, invisible, only God. When we see earthly rulers, institutions, and governments that have very real authority, we tend to forget that they are not eternal, they are not ultimate, and they will not last. The prayer in 1 Timothy 2:1-4 reminds us to respect those in authority, but it also reminds us where authority truly comes from.

Jesus said that all authority in heaven and on earth is His,[10] but in His divine design, God allows humanity to be stewards of that authority. This is why prayer for governmental leaders is vital; wherever there is a concentration of power and authority, there will inevitably be intense spiritual warfare. When authority is abused or misused, we can rightly criticize those who abuse their power. Ultimately, there is a spiritual battle taking place, and it is not human authority but God's authority being indicted. The church must get involved and pray. After all, Jesus said that the gates of hell will not stand against the church.[11]

What Should I Pray for Leaders?

Thinking of leaders first of all as people reminds us that they face challenges just like everyone else. Often, those challenges are not always related to the specific function of their position. Whether someone is a leader serving in elected office or not, the sort of character and integrity needed most in our day is typically developed through times of difficulty, personal challenges, and, often, tragedy. Think back to a time when you faced a difficult challenge or personal tragedy and what was required to get through it. Was it the support of family and friends? Did you need wise counsel from a trusted mentor? Perhaps the things you most needed were understanding and a little grace from the people around you. These things are also what I mean by the more we can ask *for* leaders.

The remainder of this section of the book is the product of years working at the Oklahoma State Capitol and as a pastor in the Washington DC area. Answering this last question, *what should we pray*, has required more than a decade of contemplation, study, and practice. It also required building long-standing friendships with elected leaders at the national, state, and local levels—friendships for which I'm truly thankful, with leaders on whose behalf I'm happy to offer intercession and prayer. It is an incredible privilege to walk alongside elected leaders in their task as legislators. I do this bringing no other agenda than to express gratitude for their service and leadership in the state and to pray for them.

Throughout this time, I have offered public invocations at official events and at the opening of dozens of legislative sessions. The transcripts of some of those prayers are on the pages of Chapter 7. Sharing them was the original inspiration for writing this book, for the purpose of giving an example of various ways you can pray for leaders. I have known a few people who were truly anointed in the way they pray, and I don't necessarily count myself as one of them. But everyone can pray. The past many years have afforded me the unique opportunity to pray in the specific context of a state capitol and for government leaders. These prayers on the pages that follow are recorded in the hope that they might be helpful examples for how any of us can pray for leaders and our nation.

Believing that leaders matter should produce a desire for leaders to be better. One of the first conversations I had when launching my work in the state capitol was with the senior leader of one of the largest Christian denominations in Oklahoma. It was a very encouraging conversation as we spoke at length about the importance of prayer for leaders. A statement from that conversation cemented in my mind. I honestly cannot remember exactly who said it or if it was a mixture of what we both shared, but here it is: when our leaders are better, we are all better. I believe that is true and helps me to know what we really should desire *for* leaders: desire that their lives, homes, and families will be blessed. I pray that our leaders are blessed so that we all may be.

Chapter 6

★ ★ ★ ★ ★

Because We All Can Pray

*The ministry of prayer is the most important service
that the Church of Christ can engage in.*

—D. Edmond Hiebert[1]

A Human Endeavor Common to All People

When legislators adjourn from the legislative session, leave the Capitol building, and are busy with the many other aspects of their life, I spend much of my time speaking across the state and encouraging all people of prayer to understand this principle found in Scripture and to pray sincerely for leaders and their families. Before reading the various examples of prayers for leaders in the next chapter, take a moment and consider this one human endeavor that can be common to all people: *prayer.*

Teaching his reader to pray for those in authority, Paul reminds us that we have access to the most extraordinary power and spiritual resource available on earth. Perhaps the most prevalent need among Christ followers in our generation, and all people, is a deeper understanding of the power of prayer. As you read the many examples of prayer for leaders on the following pages, consider the nature and power of prayer.

As previously stated, the prayers described in 1 Timothy were meant to be from an attitude of giving thanks for those who lead and to intercede on their behalf. But remember the comment from David Pawson, that for all the good democracy has brought to our world—and democracy has brought enormous good—it has also resulted in a tendency for people to lose the ability to respect their leaders.[2]

I regret that is probably truer than I wish to admit. My sincere endeavor is to both pray for leaders and encourage others to pray as Paul wanted his readers to pray for their leaders, with thanksgiving and making intercessions. I know that is almost impossible when we do not really know our leaders or when we distill leaders down to mere representations of the specific policies they promote or, more often, their political party. By doing this, we forget they are ultimately people on a journey of public service and faith. But what does prayer really do?

Prayer Helps Us to Know Others

To pray is to humble yourself before God and others. The discipline of prayer keeps us from responding to people and situations before taking the time to fully understand them. Here is what I mean: my natural inclination is to quickly defend whatever default positions I hold, as well as the principles that led me to them. *Defend* is the right word because we rarely consider our own positions in a vacuum. Instead, I see them as under threat from opposing points of view, and in those moments, I become angry. There is a real problem with this tendency. Remember Proverbs 21:2: "All a person's ways seem right to him, but the Lord weighs hearts." As this ancient wisdom warns, there is a deep corruption in the human heart. However noble and selfless I believe myself to be, there is a taproot of self-centeredness and self-interest running deep in my own heart. This root of pride and selfishness runs deeper than I care to imagine. That means I'm not always aware of how it affects my positions or principles. I'm also not always aware of the anger that is lying just below my thinking.

This is why King David writes in the nineteenth Psalm, "Moreover, keep your servant from willful sins," meaning the propensity to selfishness he knows, but also, "Cleanse me from my hidden faults."[3] Rather than merely reacting, prayer gives me a moment to calm my own heart and mind and reflect. In prayer, I can take time to search my heart or, better, ask God to search my heart for me so I can honestly say that perhaps my way, as right as it seems to me, isn't as noble or selfless as I think. Prayer quiets the soul and allows anger to subside.

When that happens, I am ready to hear another person's position and really understand it. More important, I am ready to hear another person's story and really empathize with all the reasons they think and believe the way they do. I don't abandon my own principles or convictions, but I can hear the merit and value of the principles and convictions of someone else. That is one of the marks of real wisdom.

The book of Proverbs goes to great lengths to teach us that no one person has it all figured out. Each of us, even the best of us, only sees in part what is good, true, and beautiful. Prayer humbles and reminds us that we need each other, and we can and should embrace and incorporate the diversity of perspectives, experiences, and wisdom of others in order to gain the fullest understanding of wisdom and knowledge for any situation, consideration, policy, or debate.

Prayer also unites and breaks down barriers, even if it doesn't resolve differences. The environment is transformed when a group of people, who are all different and see things in different ways, stops and prays together. Whether or not we agree, disagreement can be held in peace and navigated with respect. When I invite a group of legislators to stand and pray, some may agree with much or all that was previously said or argued, and others may not. In either case, there is something about bowing our heads together in a quiet moment of prayerful reflection where none of that really matters anymore. We are then all just people. No one is greater or less than anyone else. We stand together, *willing the best* for one another before ourselves.

Prayer Helps Us to Know Ourselves

Everyone is capable of being overly confident in their own ability, especially leaders. That can create distorted self-perception, the worst kind of deception there is. As strong and powerful as we may very well be, we are finite and limited. There is only so much we can do in our own ability, and this is universally understood when we remember that everyone is susceptible to pain, frailty, and death. This is partly why Ecclesiastes 7:2 says, "It is better to go to a house of mourning than to go to a house of feasting, since that is the end of all mankind, and the living should take it to heart." We don't like to think of our own mortality. I would rather be at a party, ignoring that very fact. When confronted by pain, grief, frailty, and mortality, we think more clearly—or at least more intentionally—about the deeper realities of life and of ourselves.

In recent times, whenever there is a mass tragedy, either through an act of natural disaster or the worst kinds of violent evil from human hands, we quickly hear or read the phrase "thoughts and prayers," such as, "Our thoughts and prayers are with the victims and their families." There is growing cynicism and criticism of this response. I understand the growing frustration, and I am not arguing that prayer is the only response we can have. But in times of tragedy or pain that is beyond any one person to resolve, prayer is the right response because prayer is the path to healing for two of the most universal of human conditions: sickness and death.

As a pastor, one of the most common requests I encounter is to pray for healing. Often it is physical healing, but it can also be emotional or spiritual healing. James, the half-brother of Jesus and great leader of the first century church in Jerusalem, writes, "Is anyone among you suffering? He should pray. Is anyone cheerful?

He should sing praises. Is anyone among you sick? He should call for the elder of the church, and they are to pray over him, anointing him with oil in the name of the Lord."[4]

James goes on to write, "The prayer of faith will save the sick person, and the Lord will raise him up; if he has committed sins, he will be forgiven."[5] James then writes what is perhaps the most important and neglected concept about the nature of prayer and healing ever made. He writes, "Therefore, confess your sins to one another and pray for one another, so that you may be healed."[6]

James envisioned the church as a community of people who prayed boldly for one another and witnessed healing. Has this been your experience? I have no doubt that some who are reading this would say yes. For many others, you would say no. I admit, this has not always been my experience, and James teaches us why. We should not go directly to his comment, "Pray for one another," while ignoring the first part, "Confess your sins to one another."

I get it! I don't have any difficultly confessing my sins to God. I can do that privately, and no one has to know. I also don't have any difficulty trusting that God will forgive me. How many verses have I read in the Bible that promise God is gracious, full of lovingkindness and mercy, and faithful to forgive? According to the Christian tradition, God went to enormous lengths and Jesus died on the cross to prove that God loves me and will forgive me.

I believe God will forgive me, but I'm not sure that you will. If truth were to be told, were you to confess your sins to me, I'm not sure I would forgive you—especially if I have only my own strength and ability to rely upon. Prayer helps me to see my faults and mistakes rather than try to justify or ignore them. Prayer humbles us and reminds us that we are not perfect, and no one is.

We are first and foremost supposed to be a fellowship of *forgiven* people. Prayer reminds us of that. To be forgiven and to forgive is the greatest healing I could ever hope to know. In this regard, my strength or ability is meaningless. Who am I, really? I am someone who is forgiven, and there is more power in forgiveness than any I could hope to possess by any other means.

If we confess our sins, God is faithful to forgive.[7] In this way, God is already pouring out His healing throughout the world. I pray that the land in which I dwell is marked by a fellowship of forgiven and forgiving people.

Prayer Helps Us to Know God

Last, prayer draws us closer to God. Prayer allows us to see ourselves, as well as other people *and* their circumstances, the way God does. Jesus taught His disciples to pray for God's glory and kingdom to expand on earth *as it is* in heaven.[8] If I want God's glory and kingdom to come to earth, I have to first understand how God's glory and kingdom looks in heaven, and that begins with prayer.

Through what is written in the Bible and through my own experience with prayer, I believe that God hears us when we pray, and He answers. As I wrote earlier and learned from the nineteenth Psalm, I confess I do not always know the wickedness in my own heart. Being blind to my own hidden faults makes it very difficult to just turn away from evil. I must have a fixed point of ultimate good to turn toward. Prayer is the humble declaration of my soul that God's face, God's Word, and God's nature are my life's pursuit. That is how prayer helps us to know God.

A.W. Tozer said, "When the eyes of man looking out in prayer meet the eyes of God looking in, Heaven has begun here on earth."[9] I pray that it begins in the heart of each person reading this. Pray to know others. Pray to know yourself. Pray to know God. Now pray for all people and for all those who are in authority. Ask more *for* your leaders.

Chapter 7

★ ★ ★ ★ ★

Invocations from a Capitol Chaplain

Prayer for Oklahoma Governor Kevin Stitt at the Inaugural Prayer Service

January 15, 2019

Heavenly Father,

We pause in this moment, filled with anticipation for all that lies before us and our state. We are in the first day of new beginnings, new leadership, new opportunities, and also unknown, new challenges. In this world, Jesus told us, we will have many troubles. But be of good cheer, for Jesus has overcome this world. For Governor Stitt and all who now lead our state:

- The challenges are complex, but by God's wisdom, leaning not on their own understanding, may they find solutions.

- The trials before them are real, but by God's power, they will produce endurance, strength for future storms.

- The mandate remains, to cultivate the earth, seeking the welfare of this city and cities across our state, and by God's grace, servant leaders rise to the task.

Specifically, for Governor Stitt, I ask in this moment that You would quiet his mind, still his heart, and let him count the cost of what will be required of him each day over the next four years. Pour out Your love on him and Your protection over his family. Inspire him with the convictions that led him to seek this office but also make him aware of his limitations and needs.

Proverbs goes to great lengths to teach us that no one person has it all figured out, that all of us, even the best of us, still see only partly what is good, true, and beautiful. We need one another. Governor Stitt will need the perspectives of other leaders and lawmakers, as well as their knowledge and wisdom. He will need to lean on the strength of his family and others.

Mostly, he will need grace and the faithful prayers and intercessions of the people. So, Lord, let us be obedient to the scripture that commands Christians, and I invite all people of prayer to join us in this spirit of intercession.

We pray for Kevin, and all our leaders, because he will need something that no person can give him. Our nation was founded upon the belief that even in the greatest of human endeavors, humanity depends upon a sovereign and holy God for wisdom and protection, for grace and mercy, and for justice and good government.

In the Apostle Paul's letter to the church in Rome, he reminds the Christians gathered there to be subject to the governing authorities over them—because they are instruments of God. The government is not the same thing as the church, but the Bible still calls those who lead in government "servants of God."

So, as Your servant, may Kevin Stitt's time in office be marked less by political wins or legislative accomplishments and marked more by an encounter with the divine God of the universe; by a deeper understanding of his role as a public servant, with greater reverence for things that are on the heart of God (peace, joy, patience, kindness, self-control, preferring the good of others before himself);

more by justice and mercy; by ministry to the marginalized; and by visiting the widow and orphan in their affliction. With such wisdom, he will lead us well.

In the name of Jesus Christ, I pray. Amen.

A Prayer for Unity on the National Day of Prayer, Oklahoma House of Representatives

May 3, 2018

Heavenly Father,

Thank You for the gift of this day, to gather in this place. Lord, we thank You for the gift of rain to refresh our land, and we respect the incredible power of the weather. Lord, for those suffering damage or loss from the damaging storms this week, we ask for You to provide for them. We also pray for safety and protection in the days and weeks ahead. At this time of year in our state, we have regular reminders of the incomprehensible creative power contained within these three words: "let there be."

At Your Word, the universe—in all its awesome and destructive power—moved from chaos to order, and You called it good. Power was held in perfect control. Integrity and peace reigned, but in a mystery we cannot fully comprehend, deep within the human heart and in the obvious evidence of Your sovereignty, we rebelled against You, God, and peace was shattered.

God, on this National Day of Prayer, across our great country, in statehouses like ours and in the nation's capital, people are praying for *unity*. That is the theme ascribed to this day of prayer.

Lord, we join in their prayer and petition Your throne of grace to do a mighty work of reconciliation in our land. Lord, teach us what it will actually take to achieve unity. More is required of each of us than we know. And what is it that we must bring to this effort?

- Leadership, for leaders inspire us toward unity.

- Vision, for without it we are scattered.

- Justice, for there can be no real unity where people suffer unjustly.

- Mercy, for we are often blind to the depth of our own part in division.

But what is actually required to attain true unity is a radical humility beyond our wildest imagination. We must do absolutely nothing out of selfish ambition or vain conceit. We must look first to the interest of others.

If these words hang hollow in this chamber, it's not difficult to see why. The division in our nation is very real. People are bitterly divided and disdainful of anyone who does not agree with them, typically in matters that are not as important as they think.

But there are real divisions, rooted in deep wounds of offense on one side, the other, or both. We are divided by politics, by economics, by race, by religion. Families are broken; fathers have walked out on their sons and daughters. Depression and anxiety plague our generation. People are literally warring within their own soul. Can unity really come?

Yet, all these divisions pale in comparison to the greatest division in all of the universe. They are insignificant and of little consequence compared to the break in unity between humanity and God. What is impossible is for sinful humanity to approach Holy God: for who can ascend Your holy hill? No one can. No man or woman, for with man, it is impossible. But God! With God all things are possible. God demonstrated radical humility, beyond our wildest imagination, by offering us these gifts:

- *Leadership* through being a servant of all

- *Vision* of a holy, unified, redeemed humanity living in peace

- *Justice* for every offense ever committed

- *Mercy* through the forgiveness of our sins

In Jesus, the most impossible unity of all is made possible. We are united with God.

So, what, then, of every other division wreaking havoc in communities across our nation? God, You are seated on the throne saying, behold, I am making all things new. The awesome power of God is again on display with three words: let there be.

Let there be forgiveness.

Let there be grace.

Let there be humility.

Let there be love.

Let there be unity.

Amen.

A Prayer for Rest, Oklahoma House of Representatives

March 22, 2018

Heavenly Father,

Thank You for these members and the work of this week. I ask You to give strength, wisdom, and skillfulness in the work that is before them this day.

As we look to the weekend, many turn their attention to the things they were forced to set aside so they might serve in this legislature, responsibilities in their jobs, homes, and communities. But I ask, Lord, that each find the opportunity to truly rest.

Your Word says:

Remember the Sabbath day, to keep it holy: You are to labor six days and do all your work, but the seventh day is a Sabbath to the LORD your God. You must not do any work— you, your son or daughter, your male or female servant, your livestock, or the resident alien who is within your city gates. For the LORD made the heavens and the earth, the sea, and everything in them in six days; then he rested on the seventh day. Therefore the LORD blessed the Sabbath day and declared it holy.[1]

You gave the Sabbath for our good:

1. As an opportunity to stop from the work done and to consider that which is good and that which is not. Then to seek wisdom for what to do next.

2. To meet God in rest. We rest because You rested. Not out of need but to institute a rhythm to life, a way we can pattern our lives after God. Rest is perhaps one of the truly divine activities we can do.

3. To declare truth to our soul. We are not God, who does not slumber nor sleep. We are limited, finite, and frail. We need rest. Speaking truth is for our good. Denying it only does us harm.

God, the work in the week to come is weighty. So, restore these members. Refresh them, body, mind, and soul.

To You, oh, Lord, we pray. Amen.

A Prayer for Wisdom and Perseverance, Oklahoma House of Representatives

March 26, 2018

Heavenly Father,

Thank You for the gift of this day as we gather together in this chamber. Thank You for these representatives, chosen and sent to this legislative body for the very task that is before them now. Protect their homes and families as they are away.

I ask You to give both strength and patience. Lord, grant them wisdom and surround them with good counsel, with those who are both knowledgeable and humble.

As King David says of wisdom and wise counselors:

Do not be distracted by those who do wrong . . . Refrain from anger and give up your rage . . . Do not be agitated—it can bring only harm.

Trust in the LORD and do what is good . . . Dwell in the land and live securely.

Commit your ways to the LORD; trust in him, and he will act, making your righteousness shine like the dawn, your justice like the noonday.

Be silent before the LORD and wait expectantly for him.[2]

God, in this moment of stillness and quiet, we wait on You. Please fill these representatives with peace, quiet confidence, and selfless determination in the work of this week. This, in the name of Jesus, I pray. Amen.

A Prayer for God's Presence, Oklahoma House of Representatives

March 19, 2018

God, we pause in the midst of this day, very near the half-way mark in this 2018 legislative session, and in the quiet of this place, we consider how far we've come, the work that has already been done.

The Hebrew king of old writes:

The Lord looks down from heaven; he observes everyone.

He gazes on all the inhabitants of the earth from his dwelling place. He forms the hearts of them all; he considers all their works.[3]

Lord, I believe that is true. You are not distant or disinterested, but You see the interactions, negotiations, and conversations . . . the advocacy, the policy making, and the difficult decisions being made.

The work done in this chamber, for the people of our state, is not hidden from You. Neither are the hearts and minds of every member of this House of Representatives. You see each and every one—and You love them with an unfailing love.

God, I thank You for each and every one. They are a gift to us, and they serve, not just because they were elected but because they are uniquely equipped and appointed to serve at this time. I ask You to bless them. If any are ill, may they be strengthened and healed. If any are burdened by trials at home, may You give grace sufficient for this day and bless their families and their homes.

Now, Lord, as each one looks away from the work that has been done and turns their gaze to the work that lies before them in the second half of this session, God, let the leaders in this chamber hear the wisdom from this ancient king:

A king is not saved by a large army; a warrior will not be rescued by great strength . . . But look, the LORD keeps his eye on those who fear him—those who depend on his faithful love to rescue them from death and to keep them alive in famine. We wait for the LORD; he is our help and shield. For our hearts rejoice in him because we trust in his holy name.

May your faithful love rest on us, LORD, for we put our hope in you.[4]

Amen.

A Prayer for God's Protection in Times of Difficulty, Oklahoma House of Representatives

March 21, 2018

God almighty, the psalmists of old called You Lord of Hosts and declared, "God is our refuge and strength, a helper who is always found in times of trouble. Therefore, we will not be afraid."[5]

One way to read this promise is that God is a helper who is abundantly available in tight spaces.

Lord of Hosts, that is my prayer for each member of this House of Representatives. May they be protected and strengthened. May they be filled with courage and made fearless.

And may they find in You help that is abundantly available, even in the tightest of spaces—where there seems to be no way. Most often, the troubles we face are of our own doing. We back ourselves into a corner and then fruitlessly look to ourselves to find the way out. Rather, as the psalmist writes, we need only to "Be still and know that you are God."[6]

Your wisdom is knowable; Your provision is available. Let us look to You. In the stillness, may we have patience, gentleness, peace, and joy. Let each member speak with knowledge and skill, and may each hear and learn from one another.

And bless the work they do as they cooperate and negotiate. May they chart a path forward that is both just and prudent so that all may flourish and prosper in the days to come and years ahead.

This, in the name of Jesus, I pray. Amen.

A Prayer Recognizing the God of All Comfort, Oklahoma House of Representatives

March 11, 2019

Our heavenly Father,

It is good to be in this place. I pray for this legislative body and the work that they have before them. We approach You, God of all comfort and wisdom, from whom every good and perfect gift comes. We gather in this chamber with gratitude in our hearts but also with great need for Your mercy and comfort.

Lord, I know that there are those in our state facing sorrows, trials, and grief as well. As we continue in this season of lent, I am reminded of that moment Jesus was hanging on the cross and offered wine—not just to quench His thirst but what was probably drugged to ease His most certainly unbearable pain. But Christ refused.

Lord, let us remember that moment that Christ refused to dull the pain. That moment of refusal reverberates throughout history and demands that it is a lie when we are told that religion is nothing more than an opioid for the masses. That moment of refusal demonstrates that God knows that the suffering in this world is real. That moment of refusal declares that God is not only the giver of great comfort to those in pain, but God also confronts our very grief and sorrow head on. He will not leave us to face it alone. He quickens to the side of those who are brokenhearted. Thy rod and thy staff still comfort us. He surrounds us with His love.

And that moment of refusal demands that God restores, redeems, and will one day make right every wrong. That's why the psalmist can write that God has turned mourning into dancing and that sorrow is replaced with joy. God, it's beyond our ability to see or understand when tragedy strikes, but we trust that You love each and every person and every family more than we can know.

So, we ask You, God, to hold them in Your hands. Surround them with people who will love and care for them. Be the God of all comfort, as You say You are. Carry us all each day into greater hope for the time when our sorrow is finally and forever turned into joy.

In the name of the Father, I pray. Amen.

A Prayer to Remember that God Cares for People, Oklahoma House of Representatives

March 12, 2019

Father,

It is good to be in this place today. Lord, I thank You for every one of these representatives, their lives, their families, the work that they do, and all that they sacrifice to do it.

Lord, I pray now the prayer of an ancient king: "The earth and everything in it, the world and its inhabitants, belong to the Lord. For he laid its foundation on the seas and established it on the rivers."[7]

God, the work that will be done in this place in the days and in the weeks to come affect so many. Lord, remind us that it is Yours and the people are Yours. The world is Yours. The state is Yours.

Though authority and power and influence are held in this chamber, they are but stewards of it. So, may they steward it well but not hold it too tightly. Let us trust You in all that we do.

In Jesus' name I pray. Amen.

A Prayer for the Hearts of Those Who Lead, Oklahoma House of Representatives

April 1, 2019

Father,

We read in Proverbs 27:19 that as water reflects the face, so the heart reflects the person.

God, I pray for the hearts of these leaders here today. May they be humble and self-searching. May they be comforted in hurt. May they be strong and incensed by what is wicked and courageous to pursue that which is good. May they be just but also kind. And may the work that is done in this chamber and this House this week prove the hearts of these elected leaders.

We give thanks for them and pray for them with all our hearts as Your Word instructs. I pray this in the name of the God of all comfort and love, who searches our hearts.

Amen.

A Prayer to Persevere, Oklahoma House of Representatives

April 2, 2018

Heavenly Father,

Thank You for this day and the sacred privilege to gather in this chamber. Thank You for these representatives, chosen and sent to this legislative body for the very task that is before them now. Protect their homes and families as they are away.

I ask You to give both strength and patience. Lord, grant them wisdom and surround them with good counsel. And today we are indeed blessed as the voices of many teachers are heard throughout this building. May we hear now from one more, Qoheleth, an ancient king in Jerusalem: "In the day of prosperity be joyful, but in the day of adversity, consider: God has made the one as well as the other."[8]

Therefore, "Don't let your spirit rush to be angry, for anger abides in the heart of fools . . . [But remember that] the end of the matter is better than its beginning; a patient spirit is better than a proud spirit."[9]

God, in this moment, and at this point in the legislative session, we are neither at the beginning nor end of the matter but in the midst of it. God, I ask You to impart—by Your power, through Your presence, and according to Your promises—a patient spirit filled with the peace, quiet confidence, gracious compassion, and selfless determination to each member of this House of Representatives for the work of this week. And may the work done this day be for the flourishing of all families in communities throughout our state, until we reach the end of the matter.

This, in the name of Jesus, I pray. Amen.

A Prayer for Joy and Strength, Oklahoma House of Representatives

April 3, 2018

Great and gracious God,

You are seated enthroned in the heavens. Be high and lifted up and so exalted in our hearts. Let it be as the psalmist writes:

Lord, your word is forever; it is firmly fixed in heaven. Your faithfulness is for all generations; you established the earth and it stands firm.

If your instruction had not been my delight, I would have died in my affliction. I will never forget your precepts, for you have given me life through them.[10]

I give You thanks and praise You for each of these representatives, members of this body, servants of the people of Oklahoma and of Your sovereign will.

As they walk in the responsibilities of leadership, in making good legislation, debating and discerning the path forward for our state, draw to their mind the joy, even in the struggle. Give them confidence in the foundations You established. Help us all to trust in Your faithfulness from generation to generation.

May they find a strength that is beyond their own and a wisdom that is true, tested, and timeless.

This, in the name of Jesus, I pray. Amen.

A Prayer for Direction, Oklahoma House of Representatives

April 5, 2018

Our God and Father,

From whom every good and perfect gift comes. We pause in this moment at the end of this week and before the work that is to be done this day to remember You: Your unfailing love; Your faithfulness from day to day; Your victory over sin and death; the redemption, forgiveness, and peace that comes at the name of the Lord.

I thank You for each of these representatives, duly elected, sent, and serving in this legislative body. In the midst of many voices, there is often confusion and misunderstanding. In Your grace, You have called out these 101 voices to come together and speak with sincerity, clarity, and conviction and to navigate the way forward for the benefit and flourishing of all in our state. As they continue in this task, give them strength and renew them in body, mind, and soul.

And may they depend on You as the psalmist did:

Make your ways known to me, LORD; teach me your paths. Guide me in your truth and teach me, for you are the God of my salvation; I wait for you all day long.

Remember, LORD, your compassion and your faithful love, for they have existed from antiquity.

Do not remember the sins of my youth or my acts of rebellion; in keeping with your faithful love, remember me because of your goodness, LORD.[11]

In the name of Jesus, I pray. Amen.

A Prayer for God's Blessings, Oklahoma House of Representatives

April 6, 2018

Father in heaven,

In the still of this moment, flood our hearts and minds with Your rich blessings:

Mercy for those undeserving.

Grace for those most needing.

Wisdom for those asking.

Peace that is beyond understanding.

Also, You have blessed us with this nation and our state, with a representative democracy, and this legislative body.

I thank You, God, for each of these representatives, servant leaders of diverse backgrounds and experience, skills, and expertise. Bless them all, especially in the task before them. Guard their homes and bless their families.

Meet them in the very moment of every need.

I pray for them with the same confident cry of God's blessing found in Psalm 119: "Remember your word to your servant; you have given me hope through it. This is my comfort in my [frailty]; Your promise has given me life."[12]

This, in the name of Jesus, I pray. Amen.

A Prayer for Wisdom from God's Word, Oklahoma House of Representatives

April 11, 2018

Oh, great King of the Ages, the immortal, invisible, and only wise God,

To You and You alone belong all glory and honor and dominion, forever. Thank You that You have not left us without a witness to Your nature, Your character.

You are a good God, and You delight in salvation. You are a redeemer of lives and relationships—first of all a relationship with You. Thank You for comforting those who mourn; there is something about the God of the Bible that quickens to the side of the broken-hearted. Be especially near to the family of Representative [name omitted] in this time of loss and grief at the death of a member of their family. There are others on our minds that we know need Your comfort today.

The scripture says that "for as heaven is higher than earth, so my ways are higher than your ways, and my thoughts than your thoughts."[13]

But this does not mean God confuses or misleads us. By no means does God turn passions against another person. Surely, You are a God of order, of peace, of wisdom, of reconciliation, and of revelation.

At the very word of God, order forms from chaos, light pierces darkness, life springs up from death, and anger bows down to lovingkindness.

And Your Word invites us to know You:

- To read Your Word is to know the mind of God.
- To trust Your Word is to know the love of God.
- To love Your Word is to know the heart of God.
- To obey Your Word is to know the will of God.

God, I am thankful, and I pray for every member of this legislative body. May they look to You and Your Word and find grace sufficient for this day. May they consider it pure joy when they face trials of various kinds. May they ask for Your wisdom and know You give it freely and without reproach.

Then, may they work with charity and goodwill toward one another. May the work they do this day be blessed and cause the flourishing of all in Oklahoma.

Hear our prayer, oh, Lord. Amen.

A Prayer for Joy, Oklahoma House of Representatives

April 21, 2018

Father in heaven,

In the still of this moment, flood our hearts and minds with Your rich blessings.

I thank You, God, for each of these representatives—servant leaders of diverse backgrounds and experience, skills, and expertise. Bless them all, especially in the task before them. As they meet, we place their homes and their families in Your care and ask You to guard and bless each one.

Meet them in the very moment of every need.

Today, I pray for these members, that they would have joy—sustaining and abiding joy, the joy that the prophet Isaiah discovered:

> I will give thanks to you, Lord, although you were angry with me. Your anger has turned away, and you have comforted me. [Indeed,] God is my salvation; I will trust him and not be afraid, for the Lord, the Lord himself is my strength and my song. He has become my salvation and with joy, I will draw water from the well of salvation.[14]

God, I pray they discover again Your joy. Amen.

A Prayer for Confidence in the Future, Oklahoma House of Representatives

April 30, 2018

God in heaven, Lord of all,

The psalmist writes, "May God be gracious to us and bless us; may he make his face shine upon us, so that your way may be known on earth, your salvation among all nations."[15]

In the final days of this fifty-sixth legislative session, we reflect upon this House of Representatives and all they have endured, all they have accomplished, as well as those things left undone that leave their hearts burdened for future days and sessions.

It is easy, God, to set our focus solely upon the politics or policy outcomes, the victories and defeats, the progress—sometimes swift and sometimes slow.

It is easy because policies matter. The work done in this Capitol by this legislative body makes a difference and will impact individuals, families, and communities across our state. They are not insignificant to You. So, I pray that the policies enacted in this session bless all who are in our state and cultivate human flourishing.

It is easy to look just at politics or policies and ignore the people involved. This is surely a sickness in our day. One thing I know for sure is that the people in this chamber are not insignificant to You.

But, God, I give You praise and thanks for *these* members of *this* Oklahoma House of Representatives. As legislators and lawmakers, they are servant leaders who have and continue to set an example for civility and grace, not compromising their convictions but extending a hand to honor one another and work together to lead our state.

God, bless these members in the work before them this day. Where they fall short, give them grace and humility to seek forgiveness and to forgive. And let them persevere to the finish.

It is easy, finally, to focus on politics or policies and forget that it is Your sovereign hand guiding the course of human history. As we read in the sixty-sixth Psalm:

Come and see the wonders of God; his acts for humanity are awe-inspiring . . . He rules forever by his might; he keeps his eye on the nations . . . He has not turned away [from us when we pray] or turned his faithful love from [us].[16]

Lord, there is no future we need fear where God is seated on the throne. This is the hope where we find confidence and faith to lead and to inspire and to leave our homes, our cities, and state better than we found them.

This, in the name of Jesus, I pray. Amen.

A Prayer for the Leadership and Protection for Families, Oklahoma House of Representatives

April 20, 2018

Our heavenly Father,

I thank You for the gift of this day and for the work You are doing in us all so that we may will and act according to Your good purpose. God, I thank You for this House, for all the members here, and I praise You for each one, for their dedication, sacrifice, and service in this legislature.

Leadership matters because the power and influence we hold is not our own; we are stewards of Your authority and power. And Your will is for the flourishing of the whole world. Scripture commands people of faith to pray with thanksgiving, making intercessions on behalf of our leaders. Lord, we do just that.

We specifically pray today for the leadership within this body. According to Your power and purposes, I pray for the Speaker of the House of Representatives and the Speaker Pro Temp. Before Your throne of grace, I pray for the minority party leaders serving this House of Representatives.

I ask that Your grace be sufficient for each one of them, that You give them an extra portion of Your peace and comfort, that You would build them up in strong confidence, with all humility and steadfastness.

Lord, we pray for their families, for their loved ones, their spouses, their children. May Your grace cover them. Wherever they are in this moment, this day, draw especially near and give Your protection. Guard their minds and hearts.

In the name of Jesus, I pray. Amen.

A Prayer for Humility on Ash Wednesday, Oklahoma House of Representatives

March 6, 2019

Our Father in heaven,

Today is Ash Wednesday, and today millions of people around the world mark this day and enter a season of prayer, reflection, fasting, and repentance. The Lenten passage today comes from the prophet Joel:

> Blow the horn in Zion; sound the alarm on my holy mountain! Let all residents of the land tremble, for the day of the LORD is coming; in fact, it is near . . . Even now, this is the Lord's declaration. Turn to me with all your heart, with fasting, weeping, and mourning.[17]

Jesus, You came into the world preaching the kingdom of heaven, and in the kingdom, it is the poor in spirit, the humble, the peacemakers, and those who mourn the weight and consequence of sin who are truly blessed.

Jesus, You preached that the great reversal, in fact, is true: the first shall be last and the greatest will become a servant of all. And, Jesus, You who are the very nature of God did just that. You humbled Yourself and became the servant of every soul who could not hide nor make their sin right.

So, God, may this day and the next forty days be filled with solemn reflection. May we feel the weight of sin. May we look to You and march steadily toward the great day of celebration, salvation, forgiveness, and joy. For God does not leave us in our sin. But the penalty God Himself has paid. Victory to us God has given.

To the God of all victory, I pray. Amen.

A Prayer of Thankfulness for the Democratic Process and for God to Bless All People, Inaugural Ball for Governor Kevin Stitt

January 14, 2019

Heavenly Father,

We are grateful to be in this place, at this time, and for this purpose. We gather as friends, thankful for a country where the people are free to choose those who lead us, thankful for the inauguration of Kevin Stitt, today, and with great hope for the future of Oklahoma.

It is good and right to celebrate and remember all we've endured and experienced to arrive at this moment, knowing that every good and perfect gift, every blessing we have, ultimately comes from You, God, the Father of Lights, in whom there is no shadow of changing.

This night, God, we pray: Bless Governor Stitt, First Lady Sarah Stitt, their six children, and entire family. Keep them and protect them. Make Your face to shine upon them and show them extraordinary grace, sufficient for each day.

Bless the state of Oklahoma. Make her prosperous and just, fair and filled with opportunity. May the prosperity of any one part of Oklahoma mean the flourishing and thriving of all in Oklahoma.

Bless our evening tonight. For this meal and the fellowship we share, we are grateful. And above all, let that which honors God tonight remain cemented in our hearts and minds, and let that which does not quickly fade.

For all we do, we do for the name that is above every name, at whose name every knee will bow and at whose name anyone can be saved.

In the name of Jesus Christ, I pray. Amen.

A Prayer Trusting in God's Purposes, Oklahoma House of Representatives

February 11, 2019

Father,

Thank You for the gift of this new day. Jesus, You taught that we could pray for God's kingdom to come on earth as it is in heaven.

Remind us—before we seek Your kingdom to advance in our nation and state, our communities and homes—to first seek Your kingdom to advance in our own hearts. It will, if we humble ourselves and ask.

I pray that a kingdom advance would come with greater peace for these members of this House of Representatives and with Your wisdom.

Looking to the work on this floor today, Proverbs 16 tells us,

The reflections of the heart belong to mankind, but the answer of the tongue is from the LORD. All a person's ways seem right to him, but the Lord weighs motives. Commit your activities to the LORD, and your plans will be established.[18]

Lord, our plans always seem right to us. We would not pursue them otherwise. But, we confess, ultimately we do not know the motives of the heart. Even our own motives can be hidden to ourselves—but You know.

So we heed wisdom's instruction. Committing our ways to You, never forgetting the promise in the very next verse: "The Lord has prepared everything for his purpose."[19]

In the name of Jesus Christ, I pray. Amen.

A Prayer of Thanks for the Opportunity to Pray, Oklahoma House of Representatives

March 4, 2019

Father,

I thank You for this day, the gift of life and breath, for health enough to serve in this Capitol, in this state and nation.

I thank You for the opportunity to invoke the creator of all things, the author of life, and the redeemer of our souls. There is perhaps no greater freedom we enjoy than the freedom of conscience and of the soul, to seek divine truth and cherish one's own hope in God, hope that sustains us and hope we can freely share with others.

God, for every person in this chamber and throughout this building, I ask that they have joy today—not a light-hearted blissfulness but a firm, secure, deeply rooted joy that will sustain them in the midst of difficult work and challenges: joy that relieves all worry, joy that replaces anxiety with peace, and peace that surpasses understanding and guards our hearts and minds.

Remind us that "You, LORD, will guard us; you will protect us from this generation forever."[20]

You are not blind to our needs or challenges. You see us clearly, and it is in Your very nature to quicken to the side of those who are most wanting. May we not be blind to the myriad of ways You work in our lives or to those people You use as agents of grace.

Thank You for the opportunity to begin this legislative day recognizing the presence of faith and the power of God in the midst of human affairs, including the legislative responsibilities before this House of Representatives.

Now, Lord, bless each member of this house. Protect and provide for their families. Each one stewards authority and leadership but serves at great personal sacrifice, and I thank You, God, for each one.

Amen.

A Prayer for Awareness of Our Limitations, Oklahoma House of Representatives

Feb. 27, 2019

Our Father in heaven,

It's good to be in this place. I thank You for each person who's made it here safely and for those who are struggling on the roads across our state. I ask for Your provision and protection for so many without homes and living day and night out in the elements.

Lord, I also thank You for the members of this body. Lord, our leaders and our representatives are, in fact, chosen servants. I pray for them that they would be encouraged and blessed and that they would be reminded and comforted with the knowledge that You hold them in Your hand and You care for them.

The psalms tell us to "Sing a song of wisdom, for God is king of the whole earth. God reigns over the nations . . . seated on his holy throne . . . For the leaders of the earth belong to God."[21]

So for these leaders before me today, Lord, where they are limited, may they know that You are limitless. Where their vision is narrow, let them know that You see clearly what they cannot.

There's always more going on and more opportunity to see, to serve, and to lead with more humility and grace. And let the song in our hearts today be that of wisdom as we serve others and give glory to You.

In the name of the Father, I pray. Amen.

A Prayer Thankful for Freedom and for Joy, Oklahoma House of Representatives

March 4, 2019

Father,

I thank You for this day, for the gift of life and breath and health enough to serve in this Capitol, in this state, and nation. I thank You for the opportunity to invoke the creator of all things, the author of all life, and the redeemer of our souls. There is perhaps no greater freedom we have than the freedom of conscious and of the soul, to seek one's truth, and to cherish one's own hope in God that sustains us, and we can freely share.

God, for every person in this chamber and throughout this building, I ask that we have joy today, that it would be a joy that relieves all worry, a joy that replaces anxiety. And give us peace—peace that passes all understanding. Remind us that You, Lord, will guard us. You will protect us from one generation to the next and on forever. You are not blind to our needs or our challenges. You see us clearly. It is in Your nature to quicken to the side of those who are most wanting. May we not be blind to the myriad of ways You work in our lives or to those people You use as agents of grace.

God, I thank You for the opportunity to begin this legislative day recognizing the presence of faith and the power of God in the midst of human affairs, including the legislative responsibilities before this House of Representatives. So bless each member of this House. Protect and provide for them and their families. Each one stewards leadership and authority but serves at a great personal sacrifice. Thank You, God, for each one.

It's in Your name I pray. Amen.

A Prayer for Military Veterans, Wreaths Across America, Oklahoma State House Ceremony

December 9, 2019

Our gracious and heavenly Father, God of all comfort and wisdom, from whom every good and perfect gift comes,

We gather this morning and join together with people across our nation, in solemn recognition of our military veterans, for each person who placed themselves in service to our nation and in many instances laid down their lives. There is a special and unique meaning and purpose that has drawn each one of us here today.

But for the next few moments and whatever our particular reason may be, all of us gather here to rehearse those things we've long believed; that the enduring price of freedom has always been measured in blood and in sacrifice.

God, we are here to remember. We remember the veterans in our own families and lives. We remember those fathers and mothers, brothers and sisters, sons and daughters. We are thankful to God for their service and sacrifice.

Father, we are here to honor. It is our duty to give honor to those whom honor is due. To lay one's life down for a friend, Jesus taught us, there is no greater love than this. For every act of courage, for every moment of valor, and for every life marked with bravery, we declare they are to receive our nation's honor and respect.

Lord, we are here to learn. The things of greatest value and the truly eternal truths in this world are rarely celebrated: humility, selflessness, integrity, gentleness, and preferring the good of the other above that of ourselves.

But of all the things we must teach our younger generations, let us teach them what is found in Scripture, "For freedom, Christ has set us free."[22]

That is why free people lay down their lives in the noble cause of bringing freedom to those who do not possess it. To preserve and promote the cause of liberty, and to fight for a more peaceful, freer, and dignified world, is a most God-like and transcendent endeavor.

For those who serve, today, in our nation's military, we pray for safety and protection. We ask as the Psalmist did, that you would be their steadfast love and fortress, a stronghold and deliverer, and a shield in whom they may take refuge.[23]

For those who rest in the eternal comfort of God's presence and love, we know they await the great harvest of righteousness that is sown in peace by those who make peace. For that price which has been paid, we thank you. For those who paid it, we thank you.

Now unto Him who once and for all paid that price, Jesus Christ, and unto the God of the Ages, eternal, immortal, the only wise God be all glory and honor, forever. Amen.

Chapter 8

★ ★ ★ ★ ★

Taming the Tongue

Devotional Message and Prayer in the First Week of the Oklahoma Teacher Walkout and Protest at the State Capitol

April 12, 2018

The letter of James was written, we believe, by the great leader of the first century church in Jerusalem and the half-brother of Jesus. In it, James describes deep spiritual maturity and spiritual strength.

The letter opens with a well-known passage: "Consider it a great joy, my brothers and sisters, whenever you experience various trials, because you know that the testing of your faith produces endurance" (or *patience*, if you have the King James).[1] The word *patience* in Greek is *hypomonen*, and it is a marvelous word. In his book, *New Testament Words*, William Barclay describes *hypomonen*. We learn from Barclay that this is not the ability of a person to retreat into the sanctuary of God—though we can, for God is our refuge and strength. It is not the protection of God that ensures our safety or deliverance—though we know that God fights our battles for us. "Rather, this is the quality that enables a person to stand on their own two feet facing the storm. The testing of faith produces in us a transcendent fortitude of the soul—to have courage and not be afraid. And the strength to stand on our own two feet facing the storm."[2]

James goes on to say, "And let endurance [patience or *hypomonen*] have its full affect, so that you may be perfect, complete, and lacking nothing."[3]

I believe with all my heart that in the journey of life and in faith, God is shaping us and molding us, pruning us and refining us. He is transforming us until the image of God—in which all people are divinely created but was fractured by sin—is finally and fully restored.

I believe with all my heart that this can and does happen for you just as much when you are here, in this legislature, about the work of the people, as it does when you are at home with your families or in your respective congregations and faith communities.

I suspect that for most of you in this body—on all sides of the issues before this body in the last few days—you have labored, you have strived, you have been tested, and perhaps you have discovered your limitations and learned to trust in others and in God a little more than you did before.

Be encouraged! God works in all things, redeems all things, and in all things a most important work of the reformation of the inner-self is in progress. It will result in a strength you never imagined you could have—for a time you could not have imagined.

James goes on in this letter, building on what spiritual strength and maturity looks like: resisting any partiality or favoritism;[4] practicing true religion, which is visiting those most marginalized in the midst of their affliction and remaining unstained by this world;[5] resisting greed;[6] resisting hatred and adultery;[7] and learning to look to others more than yourself.[8]

He makes an observation that is so subtle it can easily be missed. He writes, "For we all stumble in many ways. If anyone does not stumble in what he says, his is mature, able to also control the whole body."[9]

James says, show me a person who has tamed the tongue, and I'll show you a perfect person, mature in life and in faith, with perfect control over every aspect of their life. Perfection is, therefore, not in what you do, accomplish, or create but in what you say—more likely in what you don't say.

I suspect there is not a person in this chamber for whom that simple phrase is not a *deafening indictment*. Oh, how I have failed to tame my tongue this week. And I am sorry.

The tongue really is a restless evil, as James described, full of deadly poison.[10] Consider how a whole forest is set ablaze by such a small fire.[11]

In the Old Testament book of Job, when considering his situation and despair, Job begins to reason and to ask, what have I done to really deserve this? Then Job considers who God is, and he concludes, even if it were true that I am totally blameless and righteous, the moment I open my mouth to speak in my own defense, my tongue would betray me and condemn me.[12]

Here is one final observation from James. We ought to consider with great sincerity and seriousness how we belittle, diminish, and even abuse the extraordinary power of our own words.

We read in James that with the tongue we worship and bless our Lord, God the Father . . . and with it we also curse people who are made in God's image.[13] He says this should not be. Then James confounds us and presents us with a logical impossibility.

He gives three illustrations of natural absurdities: a saltwater spring that produces fresh water; a fig tree that produces olives; and a grapevine that produces figs.[14]

Yet, in the face of impossibility, this is exactly what happens with the tongue. There can and will be redemption. There can and will be restoration. There can and will be humility, love, and forgiveness. There can and there will be the highest of purposes for our words:

to bless the Lord, our God; to give praise to the One who is worthy of our praise.

Honorable ladies and gentlemen of the Oklahoma House of Representatives, my prayer each and every day—for every one of you—is that God will bless you and will strengthen you, that the redeemer of the world will transform your hearts first, then your minds, and that this will change the way you speak to one another to traverse the areas of disagreement and opportunities for compromise and unity.

As if the very air in this building would be changed, I pray for God to create an environment and a culture marked by spiritual strength and maturity. I pray for skillful legislators, who speak with conviction and compassion, who champion individual principles with a willingness to be convinced of another's point of view.

Finally, I pray for you to be a model of humility and integrity in governance for our state to our nation and to the world. And I thank you for your sacrifice and dedication to do it. It is my honor and privilege to pray with you and for you. May God bless you and keep you and make His face to shine upon you. Will you pray with me?

Our God and our Father,

We approach You with the gratitude of those forgiven and restored, with the confidence of those who are witnesses to Your grace and goodness, and with the boldness of the who ask first for the well-being of others before ourselves.

I ask You to build up in these representatives character, strength, kindness, and joy. Build in them the quality to stand on their own two feet to face the storms of this day and those to come.

Give them rest now and time at home with their families. Meet them in every need.

In the name of Jesus, I pray. Amen.

Ask More *of* Leaders

You don't lead by hitting people over the head.
That is assault, not leadership.

—President Dwight Eisenhower[1]

But what comes out of the mouth comes
from the heart, and this defiles a person.

—Matthew 15:18

Chapter 9

★ ★ ★ ★ ★

Who Lead with Integrity

Above all else, guard your heart,
for everything you do flows from it.

—Proverbs 4:23 (NIV)

Thinking of Leaders as People

Do leaders matter? Perhaps you're not fully convinced. But thinking better of the nature of authority and the function of authority in society suggests they do. Up to this point, believing leaders matter involves the following challenge: to better distinguish between the *position* of leadership and the *person* in that position. There is a distinction. The person is not the same thing as their position. A growing ability to separate the function of leadership from the person in a position of authority is important if we are to pursue civility, integrity, and the servant leaders we need. Where we focus our attention is another result of this approach. When the position and the person are distinct in our mind, we can apply focused attention on one regardless of the other. The difference can be subtle but always significant.

Here is why. Leaders are first of all *people*. For leaders in government, before they are politicians or elected officials, they are people on a journey of public service and leadership. The various labels of political party, the policies they promote, or the philosophies they champion fade away when we see them primarily as a person. Giving precise attention to the *people* who lead, or aspire to lead, allows us to focus on the important work of developing individuals who are not just skilled leaders but also servant leaders. However, the character-building and the instilled determination to serve others should not only be a priority for the development of future leaders. An ever-growing dedication to servant leadership and the development of strong character and integrity are just as important for people already in positions of authority. These qualities are the more we are asking *of* leaders.

We Need People of Integrity

With our attention on the people and our goal set on developing servant leaders of strong character and integrity, we can now move to the third step in the process: ask more *of* leaders. Maybe what you would like to ask of a leader pertains to a particular problem or challenge in your life or community. There are actions leaders can take and policies they can champion. It is right and appropriate to have those discussions with leaders. We need leaders who faithfully fulfill the functions of their authority. Before this, consider one more implication to thinking of leaders, first of all, as people. What we need most in a leader is that they are a person of integrity.

Being a person of integrity is the key to the third step in the process. In his book *The Making of a Leader*, J. Robert Clinton delves into the developmental phases that leaders go through. Early on, a leader should experience what Clinton calls an *inner-life growth process*.[1] He writes, "There are many lessons in the development of a leader. None are more crucial in timing or in impact that the early ones, which focus on character building."[2] In his study of leadership, Clinton notes that there is one word that really captures the essence of character: integrity.[3] The *more* that we are really asking of leaders is a well-developed character, and it will look like integrity. But what does integrity actually look like?

The chapters that follow in this section consider nine qualities most needed in a leader who has integrity. They are nine virtues common to all people and ones that we should ask of those who are leaders and those who seek to be leaders. The discussion of these nine virtues is found in Galatians 5:22-23, a well-known passage from the Apostle Paul's letter to the churches in Galatia. These characteristics are popularly called the *fruit of the Spirit.*

What follows is not intended to be a deeply theological enterprise or exhaustive exploration of the spiritual implications of Paul's writing. Rather, this is designed to inspire leaders and challenge us to think more critically of the elements of character and integrity we need in leaders today. We need leaders who are loving, who are peacemakers, and who inspire joy. We need leaders who are patient and kind. We need leaders who are good, faithful, gentle, and model self-control. When we first ask those things of leaders, then we can ask the other things.

For Freedom's Sake

Consider what Paul writes in this letter shortly before naming the fruit of the Spirit. In Galatians 5:1, Paul writes, "For freedom, Christ set us free. Stand firm then and don't submit again to the yoke of slavery."

Three simple truths are immediately evident:

1. People are not free.
2. Christ sets people free.
3. Christ sets people free for freedom's sake.

The cause of freedom is ensconced in America's DNA. The Declaration of Independence states, "We hold these truths to be self-evident, that all men are created equal, that they are endowed by their Creator with certain unalienable Rights, that among these are Life, Liberty and the pursuit of Happiness." The self-evident truths extolled by the Declaration's signatories cast a vision for a future of human dignity, equality, freedom, and opportunity, a future that many would fight and die to secure and that many since have fought and died to protect.

The framers of Declaration of Independence clearly believed freedom was a divinely endowed right but knew it was not the inherent reality of humanity. The same is true today. All around the world, we find people oppressed by forces outside themselves as governments and institutions limit their freedom. Within our own nation's history, we know that freedom is still a work in progress. In writing, "For freedom, Christ set us free,"[4] Paul also recognized the restrictions and limitations that threaten and deprive people of the divine right to be free. This passage is an enduring reminder that promoting freedom is a most Christ-like and godly endeavor.

But even if a person is blessed enough to live in a free society without external constraints to liberty, they can still find themselves in captivity and lacking the very freedom they were designed to enjoy. Jonathan Merritt, a columnist for the *Atlantic* who writes on religious issues, tweeted, "Every human is both the jailer and the inmate in their own life. We are incarcerated by our bad habits, dark tendencies, and hurtful propensities." Merritt is right.

The Last of Human Freedoms

You may be familiar with the story of Victor Frankl. Dr. Frankl was a prominent twentieth century philosopher of psychology and is best known for his contributions to what we know as existential therapy. In 1942, Frankl and his parents, wife, and brother were arrested and sent to the Thereisienstadt concentration camp; Frankl's father died there within six months. Over the course of three years, Frankl was moved between four concentration camps, including Auschwitz, where his brother died and his mother was killed. Frankl's wife died at Bergen-Belsen. When Frankl's camp was liberated in 1945, he learned of the death of all his immediate family members, with the exception of his sister who had emigrated to Australia. In the camps, Frankl and fellow prisoners made an effort to address the despondency they observed in other inmates.[5]

It was said that while in the concentration camps, Victor Frankl could predict which prisoners possessed the "quality within" to survive this atrocity. Frankl later developed a therapeutic practice based on Soren Kierkegaard's concept of *will to meaning*, and he believed that people were not driven by pleasure or passion, as other psychologists and therapists of his day asserted, but by the search for meaning.

Frankl observed, "Everything can be taken from a man but one thing: the last of human freedoms—to choose one's attitude in any given set of circumstances, to choose one's own way."[6] I've studied psychology, philosophy, and theology, and I'm no expert in any of these disciplines. But I find this truth reverberates through scripture: this last of human freedoms is, in fact, a universal grace from God that compels me to believe that God designed people to live in freedom.

The message of Jesus, His work on the cross, and the gospel proclaimed by His followers for two millennia is that the greatest experience of freedom happens within the human heart—no matter what happens around you. We never stop pursuing freedom in other arenas of society and the world, but when Paul says, Christ set us free, he means us to know that God can release in me and in you a deep freedom of the soul, the mind, the heart.

The fruit of the Spirit is a discussion about what freedom looks like. So, how does a mind or a heart that is set free look? It looks like love, joy, peace, patience, kindness, goodness, faithfulness, gentleness, and self-control.

What happens when freedom manifests in a person's life in these ways? They find deep meaning for their life and even the power to survive unbearable conditions. That meaning can be found through work and vocation, public service and politics, or by living each and every day to impact the lives of people they meet. The fruit of the Spirit is a great place to begin developing a profile of the kind of leaders we need.

People are meant to be free, and for freedom, Christ has set us free. Let's now consider what full freedom in looks like.

Chapter 10

★ ★ ★ ★ ★

Who Lead with Love, Joy, and Peace

First of the Fruits: Love

Love is the first of the fruits that Paul names. It is a word that is tossed around a lot in our culture without fully considering what is meant. Often, love can be construed as soft or delicate, something that solely belongs to the realm of human emotion. The word *love* can be easily cheapened and overused.

Every year I prepare for Valentine's Day in an unconventional way: by watching *Braveheart*. I'm serious. The story told is one of considerable love. It is a story of one man's love for a nation, his people, and his family. These days, the concept of love can be soft, trivial, or even delicate. But the love on display by the heroes of that story is one of incredible courage and ferocity as they stand up against tyranny and evil. Spoiler alert, the movie ends with the hero dying, having given his life for the freedom of those he loves. It is an obvious messianic symbol. Jesus Himself taught that the very highest form of love is to lay one's life down for a friend.

The Christian tradition and history points to the blood of martyrs, who paid with their lives for their love of God and belief that God so loved the world that He gave His son. Our culture is replete with both historical and literary figures who can be best described as *warrior poets*—those who approach love courageously and write beautifully about its power.

The definition of *love* from both the Old and New Testaments is quite different from the latest jewelry commercial. Love compels a person to prefer the good of the other. Thomas Aquinas defined love as "willing the good of the other."[1] That sort of love is self-sacrificing and costly.

Self-sacrifice and costly love is Jesus' story. Since Jesus died *in love*—His love for the Father and for the world—God both raised and exalted Him over everything. The message of the gospel is that you can now know this great love of Jesus, live forever in the riches of his love, and never truly die. Even better than that, you can also now share this love with others.

The love found in the Bible through Jesus is as courageous as it is costly. But the love described in Scripture is also beautiful. The same pen that wrote of the fruit of the Spirit also taught that "love is patient, love is kind. Love does not envy, is not boastful . . . It bears all things, believes all things, hopes all things, endures all things."[2]

It was the same pen that demanded an answer to this question:

Who can separate from the love of Christ? Can affliction or distress or persecution or famine or nakedness or danger or sword? Even if we are put to death all day long, like sheep led to the slaughter . . . No, in all things we are more than conquerors through him who loved us.[3]

My challenge to you is this: think deeply about the nature of love today. This is what Jesus challenged His disciples to do. When I think of the lives of Jesus' disciples after the events recorded in Scripture, we see *warrior poets*. John is my favorite. The first-century historian Eusebius records extraordinary events of passion and courage in John's later life.

There is one story where John had been personally investing in the life of a young man in the church. John left on a long journey, and while he was away, the young man began to fall away from his faith. He stopped associating with the church and joined a gang of thieves. These were notorious, brutal people, and when John, now an old man, returned to discover this, he was heartbroken.

The story goes that he went into the thieves' cave to find the young man. When he saw this elderly John, he was horrified because he knew the thieves would kill him for letting an outsider know the location of their hideout.

So, the young man ran. I have to think John was reminded of an earlier event in his own life. When he was praying in the garden on the night Jesus was betrayed, John gave in to fear for his own life, knowing what they wanted to do to Jesus, and he ran.

Not this time. Now, like Jesus, John doesn't run away from danger but moves toward it:

> But John, forgetting his age, pursued him with all his might, crying out, "Why, my son, dost thou flee from me, thine own father, unarmed, aged? Pity me, my son; fear not; thou hast still hope of life. I will give account to Christ for thee. If need be, I will willingly endure thy death as the Lord suffered death for us. For thee will I give up my life. Stand, believe; Christ hath sent me."[4]

The young man stops in his tracks, falls to the ground, weeps, repents, and is restored. Oh, that I would know love like John and have that sort of courage—enough that I am willing to endure death.

John had thought more deeply about the nature of love. Having done so, John wrote something about God and love that, until this point, had never been said before. In 1 John 4:8 he writes, "The one who does not love does not know God, because God is love."

Until this time, no one had said God *is* love. It wouldn't make any sense. It could be said that God loves or God demonstrates love, even that God tells us to love. But to say God *is* love—that's altogether different.

D. A. Carson gave a series of lectures entitled the *Difficult Doctrine of the Love of God.*[5] Carson talks about a love that exists in God alone. It is a love that has nothing to do with us; we are not part of it at all, but we are the eternal beneficiaries. It is this remarkable love that the Father has for the Son, the Son for the Father, the Father for the Spirit, the Spirit for the Son, and the Son for the Spirit. It is a love that is so intense that it overflows from the godhead and falls down into all of creation.

Any love you experience or witness actually originated in this love of God. Any love you receive and any love you show is not something you have to conjure up from within yourself. It already existed, and we are just stewarding this love from God. If that is what love is, we understand how James can write in his letter, "Every good and perfect gift [*actually*] is from above, coming down from the Father of Lights, who does not change like shifting shadows."[6]

Does this sound bizarre? You may think it is a strange way to think about love or a unique perspective on love, perhaps. But here is when it becomes helpful; it empowers me every time I encounter someone today, especially a person who is difficult to love. Dietrich Bonhoeffer writes, "Human love cannot love an enemy . . . one who seriously and stubbornly resists [love]."[7] I'm not left to find it within myself to somehow love others. Love is not some mysterious substance I possess by being strong, patient, or well-adjusted.

Love exists outside of me. First of all, it exists in the very nature of God, and it is overflowing into my life. Paul writes that the fruit of the Spirit is *love* because he means me to know that the love I know I need to show is a love that God provides.

For a person who wronged me, God says, you can forgive just as you were forgiven. Love keeps no records of wrongs. For the person I don't really have time for, God says, you can be a blessing for them today. It doesn't have to be big; it can be a simple act. Love is not arrogant or boastful. When I'm being overlooked, and others are taking credit I deserve, God says, I see you; I know you. Love is not self-seeking.

Consider this as you think a little more deeply about the nature of love today: much of John's writings can be summed up in a statement from 1 John 4:11-12: "Dear friends, if God loved us in this way, we also must love one another. No one has ever seen God." But John teaches, "If we love one another, God remains in us and his love is made complete in us."

Victor Hugo, the great novelist who wrote *Les Misérables*, captures this idea of love well. His character Jean Valjean, who is another warrior poet, comes to the end of his life and says, "And remember the truth, that once was spoken, to love another person is to see the face of God."[8]

Notice, it is not in receiving love but in *loving* another person that we see the face of God. It's the unseen made visible at any moment, and you don't have to wait for it. It's waiting for you to love another person.

In the end, when what you do isn't appreciated or is even mocked, God says, love anyway—because love never ends. Love is the very language of heaven that we, like toddlers, are just learning to speak.

Joy Comes in the Morning

According to the Anxiety and Depression Association of America, 18 percent of US adults are struggling with some form of anxiety.[9] Almost one-fifth of the adults reading this book, statistically speaking, struggle with some form of anxiety or depression. The night before I presented this devotion in the Oklahoma State Capitol, I learned of the third pastor to commit suicide who either I or a member of my immediate family knew personally.

It is against this reality that we read that the second fruit of the Spirit is *joy*. I want this devotional message to rekindle even the smallest spark of joy for those desperately needing it. I long for that to happen.

The ancient prophets spoke of an eternal joy that gladdens our hearts, a joy that is God's great desire for the nations to know. What is this joy? It cannot be determined by our circumstances because throughout history, and in the lives of those very same prophets, circumstances were primarily marked as difficult and filled with sorrow. Yet they never lost hope in their promised joy.

It is not a state of mind, and it can't be just a feeling. We know, intuitively, that there is a difference between happiness and joy. Joy is something deeper, more sustaining and lasting than happiness.

I need a joy that is more than a gleeful, not-quite-connected-to-reality blissfulness but a very real, intensely sustaining, established-upon-the-foundations-of-faith joy!

C. S. Lewis describes joy not as a feeling but as a longing—a desire deep within every human heart.[10] Consider joy as a longing for at least three things: a purpose, a place, and a person.

First, joy is a longing for a purpose. I desire for my life to have lasting meaning. Most of us do. Believing that the things we do have real purpose makes us able to endure pain and trial. If what we do has real purpose, we can do hard things. The reason this is true is that we have come to understand how joy is not necessarily found in where we are right now, but it is waiting on the other side. The Bible consistently presents joy as something that is both now *and* not yet. In both the Old and New Testaments, we discover that joy comes in the morning.

In a sense, we already have joy because it is set right before us. We can see it and even have the faith to believe it. But joy is also just beyond our reach, calling us forward to do the hard things. The author of Hebrews writes that it was for the joy set before Him that Jesus endured the cross and gave us the gospel.

Jesus was fulfilling God's purpose and will. What can we learn from Jesus about fulfilling God's purpose and will? First, the purposes of God are never meaningless or trivial. Second, fulfilling the will of God is something no one can do in their own strength. Jesus sweat drops of blood as He asked God to give Him the strength to complete the purpose for which God sent Him. He even asked if there was any other way for God's purpose to be accomplished. But the cross was the way, and Jesus resolved, "Not my will but Yours be done."[11]

Understanding this, the gospel message can be framed another way. Because Jesus did the hard thing God asked Him to do, we can do the hard things God asks us to do.

It was purpose greater than Himself that brought Christ joy and gave Him the strength to endure. If that is true of Jesus, it is truer still that in our longing for a purpose beyond ourselves we cannot rely on our own will or strength. The strength we need to do the really hard things comes from somewhere else. But where? One Jewish teacher said, the joy of the Lord is my strength.[12] Why not begin with the very joy of Jesus that was waiting for Him on the other side of the cross? After all, Paul writes in Philippians that we can even know the joy of sharing in Christ's suffering.[13]

Finding strength in the joy of the Lord is to know the hope that is waiting on the other side of the hard things God asks us to do. It is finding the faith to believe that joy is already ours but is also on the other side. It is both now and not yet.

Understanding that joy comes in the morning allows you to accomplish all you have to do today in such a way that the things you do are not merely good but filled with eternal purpose.

Elected leaders who craft public policy and legislation can understand this point. The things they do each day and accomplish in the course of a legislative session not only affect them but also have a very real impact on the lives of millions of people. Even so, the hard-won achievements they accomplish will not always last. There will be future sessions, elections, and people who sit in their seats. New laws will be written.

The forty-sixth Psalm speaks to the temporary nature of powerful and longstanding institutions and nations. Charles Spurgeon called Psalm 46 the "Song of Holy Confidence" and summarized the passage by writing, "Happen what may, the Lord's people are happy and secure."[14] Incidentally, Spurgeon was plagued by debilitating depression his whole life. He would be part of the one-fifth of the population experiencing depression today. It seems strange to think of Psalm 46 as a song of confidence or joy because the writer depicts a life of great pain, chaos, and strife. Based on what is written by the psalmist, even if what you do today is recorded in the history of your nation, however great an accomplishment or all the good it brings, your labor is still something that will not last. The psalmist writes that the Lord of Hosts has only but to speak and the nations topple and fall. If that is true, it is certainly a different perspective on the role of elected leaders and the policies they enact.

Elected leaders can pursue the big wins and accomplishments that are great and mighty in our own eyes. Alternatively, they can approach their work in the legislature so as to produce good in the state for every community and also achieve a greater purpose, one that will last beyond their own life. It's a matter of perspective.

In God's economy, it's typically the small things, such as little acts of kindness and compassion, that matter. That's where joy is found. Joy calls us to remember that there are good works for each of us to do today. They are works that were appointed since the very foundations of the earth were laid. Live today doing those things and you will discover joy is a longing for a life of meaning and purpose.

Second, joy is a longing for a place. Many of us find immense joy when we think about our home. For me, I think of the dinner table at my grandfather's house. It was a place that was warm, kind, and loving. It was the place where I really knew who I was and where I belonged. But even that place is gone now.

I already mentioned C. S. Lewis. We think of Lewis as a great author or as the foremost apologist of the twentieth century. He certainly was those things, but Lewis was also a professor and a scholar of Medieval literature. Lewis was an expert in the art of *story*. Lewis would say there are those stories that we read once and never again. Then there are those stories we read over and over. Those are the stories that bring us joy because they create in our minds and hearts a place. Those stories create an entire world that we long to visit, explore, and enjoy. Think about reading a story to a small child, a story which captivates their imagination and truly captures their heart. What do they say when the story ends? Read it again, Daddy! They want to go back to that place.

Lewis's good friend and colleague J. R. R. Tolkien wanted his reader to understand the longing for a place that was your true home. The protagonist of his book *The Hobbit* is taken on a fantastic adventure and given a purpose greater than himself.[15] All along the way, he longs to go back to his home. When he finally does return home, what does he find? He was pronounced dead, and his greedy relatives are dividing his estate. Even in the place where we feel most at home, we are just pilgrims. There is another place that is truly our home.

Where is that place that is my true home? Look back to Psalm 46, and you will read what I find to be the most poetic verse of all Scripture: "There is a river whose streams make glad the City of God, the holy habitation of the Most High."[16]

The imagery throughout the psalm is of a chaotic unravelling of everything that one has come to know and understand and on a global scale. The ground beneath your feet gives way, nations fall, and the mountains melt into the seas. Can I even comprehend what that would be like? It is an abstraction from reality and does violence to every perception of my own existence. Now comes the fourth verse. All the disbelief and turmoil is silenced by the image of the simplest of scenes, one that is familiar and known to my concrete-thinking brain. There exists a place, a city, and a river. The psalmist wants us to know that place is real and is our true home. There is great joy in my heart when I think of my grandfather walking along the banks of that river. Joy is a longing for a place that is my true home.

Lastly, joy is a longing for a person. To love someone, and to be loved by them, is one of the greatest joys we experience in life. Even in a crowded room of friends, we can still be lonely, which is one of the greatest sorrows. But even the greatest love of your life can let you down, disappoint you, or fail you. Sustaining joy is a longing for a person who never will.

All of the great monotheistic faiths—Islam, Judaism, and Christianity—present God to us as personal. In these faith traditions, God is a person we can know and who knows us.

Christianity understands this personal God as being triune. There is God the Father, who made me and designed me to dwell together with Him, in love, forever. That's what Paul says in the first chapter of Ephesians.

According to Christianity, God takes another step toward us. The angel appears to the shepherds declaring, "I proclaim to you good news of great joy that will be for all people," because Jesus was born.[17] The word that fills our vernacular during the Christmas season is *Emmanuel,* God with us. It's curious to me that such a significant word in Christianity is mentioned only a handful of times in the Bible.

Even more remarkable is that Jesus Himself said it was good when He told his disciples He was not going to remain in the world with them. Jesus says in John 16:7, "It is for your benefit that I go away." That is unfathomable, even wrong. If our great joy is a longing for God, and if Jesus is God with us, then what He is saying makes no sense.

He wasn't done. Jesus continues to say, "Because if I don't go away the Counselor will not come to you. If I go, I will send Him to you." Now, God takes the greatest step toward us. The Spirit of God is not just God with us, He is *God with me,* the Spirit of God residing in the heart of every person who desires, who is longing for the person of God.

Joy may not be the state of my heart or my frame of mind. Especially when joy is not the reality of my circumstances, I discover that joy is a fruit of the Spirit, and the Spirit is a friend that is closer than a brother, the One who shows me the greater purpose in every day and walks with me through the hard things. The Spirit is the guarantee of that place that is truly my home. He is the one who quiets my soul and says, "I am with you."

Peace, I Give You

The writings of Genesis emerged at a time when the world was believed to be birthed out of conflict and strife. Among the prevailing theories of the origins of existence in the ancient world were myths about the Chaos and the Void, or the Babylonian creation myth recorded in the *Enuma Elis,* which told of an epic battle between the gods Marduk and Tiamat.[18]

Against such systems of belief comes the teaching from the Abrahamic faith of a Creator God peacefully speaking the world into existence. It really was a *peaceful* speaking. According to the opening lines of Genesis, the author uses the jussive tense, a form of issuing an imperative that is marked less by what we would consider a command and more by what I call permission giving. God says, "Let there be," and it was.[19]

From the opening page of the Bible, we are introduced to a God who is a source of peace, and His active work in the world brings peace. So a Judeo-Christian understanding of the origins of the universe can be described in the following way.

At God's word, the universe came into being. The following days of creation describe how the universe, in all its awesome and destructive power, becomes ordered, and God called it good. Power was held in perfect control where integrity and peace reigned. But in a mystery we cannot fully comprehend, coming from deep within the human heart and against the obvious evidence of God's sovereignty, humanity rebelled against God, and peace was shattered.

There is an order to which peace is broken. First, peace between humanity and God is broken, demonstrated by Adam and Eve being cast out of Eden. Then, peace between people is broken as seen when Cain strikes down his own brother Abel. The rest of the Bible is a narrative that describes how God, still speaking, is restoring peace: first, peace between humanity and God and, second, among people themselves.

God uses many agents across history as ambassadors who usher in peace and reconciliation into the human condition. Peace is restored to interpersonal relationships, in family systems, and whole societies. We must all the while understand that God, Himself, is the ultimate source and giver of peace. This is why the prophet Isaiah said of the Messiah that He is the very Prince of Peace.[20] There is a kingdom of God where perfect peace reigns supreme, and there is a prince of that realm who brings peace and makes peace.

There can be a problem with organized religion. Big ideas can be distilled into rote rituals. Poetic sayings can be so overused and underappreciated that they become trite or cliché.

There was great authority and insight when Jesus taught His disciples to pray for God's kingdom to come on earth *as it is* in heaven. It was a command from a prince and a king. It was a battle cry of the heart for what this world desperately needs. Peace can be restored, and prayer is more powerful than we know in bringing peace into a situation direly needing it. It is a peace that comes from the place where peace is fully found.

Yet, calls for prayer in our day often ring hollow. It's not difficult to see why. The division and strife in our nation and world are very real. People are bitterly divided and disdainful of anyone who does not agree with them. There are real divisions which are rooted in deep wounds of offense on one side or the other—usually both. We are divided by politics, economics, race, and religion. Families are broken. Fathers have walked out on their sons and daughters. Depression and anxiety plague our generation. People are literally warring within their own soul. Can peace really come?

We should remember that all these divisions pale in comparison to the greatest barrier that exists in all of the universe. They are insignificant and of little consequence compared to the chasm that resulted when peace between humanity and God was broken by sin.

The conflicts and divisions in the world may seem impossible, but the ancient psalms teach us what *actually* is impossible. It is impossible for sinful humanity to approach Holy God: "Who may ascend the mountain of the Lord? Who may stand in his holy place?"[21] The psalmist continues by answering, only the righteous, who have clean hearts and clean hands. Great theologians and much wiser pastors than me conclude: no one can climb that hill because no one is righteous.

Righteousness, or our lack of it, is the dividing line separating us from God that makes His holy hill impossible to climb. Can this division be overcome? Not if it is up to us. The Bible teaches that is impossible, and my own track record confirms it. Is there any hope? The disciples once asked Jesus, "'Then who can be saved?' Jesus looked at them and said, 'With man this is impossible, but with God all things are possible.'"[22]

We are not without hope because the impossible is still possible with God. We may yet be able to climb that hill. Preaching on Psalm 24:3, Charles Spurgeon warned that even though Jesus taught it *is* possible, don't take a single step without the prompting of God. Spurgeon implied that not only would it be possible to approach God again but that God Himself would send someone to guide us in the proper way to go. The great preacher implored his listeners to wait on God and to "be of good courage, saying, 'I waited patiently for the Lord, for he will assuredly direct me in the path of peace.'"[23]

The impossible journey is possible when you follow the path of peace. Spurgeon continued, "Even with a guide, [you] will never gain the summit unless he marks the way. And what is the way? The way to the hill of God, you know, as well as I can tell you, is Christ himself. 'I am,' saith he, 'the way.' We begin in Christ, we must go on with Christ, we must end with Christ."[24]

God makes peace possible through the radical humility of the very Prince of Peace. Humble beyond our wildest imagination, He became a servant of all. He had a vision of a holy, unified, redeemed humanity living in peace and brought justice for every offense ever committed and mercy through the forgiveness of our sins.

In Jesus, the most impossible peace of all is made possible. We are reconciled to God. Now, my favorite cliché is truer than I thought: "I made my peace with God." However, the gospel helps me understand that it is more accurate to say, "God made peace with me."

My challenge and encouragement is this: what do we do with that peace? To answer that, let me draw your attention to two key statements from Jesus. The first is in John 14:27. Jesus said, "Peace I leave with you; my peace I give to you. I do not give to you as the world gives. Don't let your heart be troubled or fearful."

We should not scoff at attempts in the world to achieve or promote peace. Never be discouraged when the methods by which people of faith promote peace are not the same, not valued, or even not preferred by the world. Jesus said it is peace that He leaves with you, and His peace is what He gives to you, but not as the world gives. His peace comes in a different way. The Bible calls it peace that is beyond comprehension.[25]

As someone who follows Jesus, I understand that peace must first reside in my own heart before seeking peace in the world—whether it is with one other person or in a family, a larger community, a legislative body, politics in general, or society. Jesus gives peace that exists even when it doesn't make sense. "Don't let your heart be troubled," Jesus told Peter, "believe in God; believe also in me."[26]

It is easier said than done. I resist peace in my own spirit all the time. Because I do, my conflicts with other people linger far longer than they should. Hear how French Catholic Theologian Father Jacques Philippe describes what inner peace looks like:

Consider the surface of a lake, above which the sun is shining. If the surface of the lake is peaceful and tranquil, the sun will be reflected in this lake; and the more peaceful the lake, the more perfectly will it be reflected. If, on the contrary, the surface of the lake is agitated, undulating, then the image of the sun cannot be reflected in it.[27]

There is an inner peace of the soul that allows a person to endure chaos and conflict around them and, more important, to reflect the peace of God into that conflict. That is what we are to do with peace. We reflect peace into the conflict that is around us. If I want to do that, then I have to go back to how I first found peace with God. Remember, Jesus said He gives peace but not as the world does. How did Jesus give me peace? He gave me peace through forgiveness. I needed it, and God gave it. In the same way, when I choose to begin with forgiveness, I discover peace within my heart and can then reflect peace.

When it comes to conflict with other people, how good and enduring it is to find peace by saying, please forgive me, or saying, I forgive you. Paul writes that the third fruit of the Spirit is *peace* because God always replaces conflict with peace when there is forgiveness.

In Matthew 5:9, Jesus said, "Blessed are the peacemakers, for they will be called sons of God." Before I am a pastor or a chaplain—and even before I am a husband and a father—I am a child of God. While the fruit of the Spirit lists a number of characteristics and traits that describe what a child of God looks like, never forget this statement of Jesus: the characteristic that most consistently identifies you as a child of God is *being a peacemaker*.

We don't just seek peace in our personal relationships, but we are to pursue peace in the whole world. God still uses agents of peace, just like before, but now we are those agents. Paul writes, we are ambassadors of Christ, and ours is the ministry of reconciliation by which God is reconciling the whole world to Himself. The fruit of the Spirit is peace, and to walk with the Spirit is to be a peacemaker.

Chapter 11
★ ★ ★ ★ ★

Who Lead with Patience, Kindness, and Goodness

Patience's Full Effect

There are a number of things that come with time, with experience, and with maturity. Among them is a certain wisdom about the things a person should pray for and a prudence about the things a person should not—at least when praying for yourself.

I'm not talking about those things we know God will not do, which are so blatantly against the nature of God according to what we reasonably know about His will. I'm also not talking about those things that we doubt whether or not God will do, the things that seem too big or too bold. We don't pray enough of those sorts of prayers.

I'm talking about the things we absolutely know, without a shadow of a doubt God *will* do. For example, a wise person knows to be careful when asking God for humility. That is a prayer God will always answer.

A pastor who mentored me early in my life learned this lesson when he pulled up to the church one Sunday morning where he was preaching for the very first time. He had just moved his family across the country to serve that church. Now, as he sat in his truck, he paused a moment to ask God for humility as a leader and their pastor. He promptly split his pants so far down the seam they had to staple them shut before he preached that first sermon.

We should, of course, pray for godly characteristics to be fashioned in our own lives, but with experience, you do learn to be very specific when you pray for them.

The next of the fruit of the Spirit is one of those things that you absolutely should pray for God to give you. Just prepare yourself before asking God to give you *patience*.

We are nearing the middle of the list of traits mentioned by Paul as the fruit of the Spirit. I should note that these are not *fruits*, in a plural sense. Rather, they are collectively one *fruit*. They present a robust picture of what God creates in the human heart. It is possible that Paul named these characteristics at random as they occurred to him, but I hold to the belief that they are ordered and build upon one another. The list begins with love, love for God and for others before yourself. This leads to joy. With love and joy, there can be a restoration of peace.

It is wise to first pray for those three things because you will need love, joy, and peace if you are about to learn patience. There are three reasons why:

1. Patience is tied to forgiveness.

2. Patience is hard.

3. Patience produces perfection.

First, *patience is tied to forgiveness*. God is principally and predominantly described in the Bible as patient. The phrase used most in the Old Testament is long-suffering. More specifically, God is slow to anger and abounding in lovingkindness.

Numbers 14:18 says, "'The Lord is slow to anger, abounding in love and forgiving sin and rebellion'" (NIV).

God's patience is inextricably tied to God's willingness to forgive. The people of God knew this was true about Him. It is why the prophet Jonah was so opposed to going to Nineveh. He is furious with God, and he actually says, "Please, LORD, isn't this what I thought while I was still in my own country? . . . I knew that you are a gracious and compassionate God, slow to anger, abounding in faithful love."[1]

And if that seems harsh to you, do a little research on the ancient Assyrians and the sheer atrocities they committed against other nations, particularly Israel. Jonah's attitude makes perfect sense and might even be justified.

But that's the whole point. God's patience is far beyond what we can fathom because even great atrocities are not beyond God's willingness to forgive.

There is real evil in the world that demands justice, and God promises that He will deal justly. But the Bible actually warns us that God's longing to forgive makes His patience so long that the world will doubt His very existence.

In Peter's second letter, he writes, "The Lord is not slow in keeping his promise, as some understand slowness. Instead he is patient with you, not wanting anyone to perish, but everyone to come to repentance."[2] He wrote that in his letter likely remembering a conversation he had with Jesus. Peter asked, "'Lord, how many times that my brother sins against me should I forgive him? Seven times?'" Jesus answered that it was "seventy times seven."[3]

Jesus meant that the patience to forgive is not about the offense or the offender, but it is a matter of the heart of the one who forgives. Growing up, I was very impatient and very hot tempered—primarily against my little brother. He wore on my every nerve. Sometimes the offenses were so insignificant they probably weren't event real. Sometimes they were.

I gained patience as I grew up, primarily through learning to forgive my brother. Here is the beauty of patience through forgiveness. Even though I haven't lived in the same city, even the same time zone, with my brother since graduating high school and we don't have nearly as much in common now that we are grown, he is one of my absolute favorite people on earth. Patience through forgiveness produces a deep love. If that's true, just how much does God love us? How much has He forgiven? How patient has He been?

We also need love, joy, and peace before gaining patience because *patience is hard*. The book of James opens by saying in verse 2, "Count it all joy, when you face trials of various kinds, because the testing of your faith produces endurance." The word for *endurance* in the King James is *patience*.

The very things in life that test our patience are what produce patience. Remember the word for patience in the book of James is *hypomonen*. Recall how commentator William Barclay describes this word not as the ability for us to retreat into the protection of God, even though we always can, nor as divine intervention in our trials, even though we know God fights our battles for us. Instead, this is God creating in you the ability to stand on your own two feet and face future storms. "It is the quality which keeps a man on his feet with his face to the wind."[4]

What could be harder work than developing an internal fortitude of the soul that allows you to stand and face future trials? It is not true that God will never give us more than we can bear. Instead, through patience, God gives us the ability to bear more than we ever thought we could.

Last, patience produces perfection. James goes on to write, "And let endurance have its full effect, so that you may be mature and complete, lacking nothing."[5] The Bible says that God, who began a good work in you, is faithful to complete it.[6] It is patience that God uses to do this. The full effect of patience is perfection, being made whole and lacking nothing. That is the destination. That is the finish line.

In 2019, the newly elected Governor of Oklahoma, Kevin Stitt, organized a relay race challenge as part of the Oklahoma City Memorial Marathon. It was the first year that an Oklahoma Governor ran in the race. The marathon is a significant event each year, where all participants run in remembrance of all those who lost their lives, those who survived, and all whose lives were changed by the violent act of domestic terrorism during the April 19, 1995, bombing of the Alfred P. Murrah Federal Building in Oklahoma City.

I was up early one morning in March of 2019 for a one-mile training run with Governor Stitt and the members of his relay team. I hate running. I've never enjoyed it, and I certainly hate waking up at five o'clock to participate in a training run for a race. However, I do *love* running races. My wife and I were not running the relay or marathon that year. We ran the 5K race. That is something we have done since the early days of our marriage, and these races are among my favorite memories, which date back to the time we lived in Washington DC and ran the 10K of the Marine Corps Marathon. There were probably forty of our friends who ran that race with us. That was the first time I learned to really love running organized races, and this love was true still when we ran the 5K in the 2019 Oklahoma City Memorial Marathon.

Here is what I love about running races. It is absolutely a competitive sport, but I'm not competing with other people. I'm competing with myself. I am trying for a better pace, a better time, and better health. The finish line is mine and only mine. There are those select few individuals who actually win marathons. I cannot pretend to understand what the finish line means to them. But for the rest of us, the finish line really is unique and uniquely yours. What God is doing in your life is different from His work in everyone else's. No wonder Paul loved to refer to a race.[7] It really is the best metaphor for life.

The author of Hebrews says, run the race marked out for you. Run your race. But run your race with endurance.[8] You guessed it. The word for *endurance* in these verses is the same word: *patience*. The best part of the race is when you first come in sight of the finish line. You start to hear the excitement and the voices of all the people cheering you on. Some are your friends, who went on and finished their race ahead of you, and many are people you've never met.

God will be standing there, too. The key to a loving, joyous, peaceful patience, which is able to endure any present difficulty, is keeping your sight on the destination. Keep your eyes on the finish line and the One who stands their waiting, Jesus, the author and perfecter of your faith.[9]

Beauty in Simple Kindness

Continuing through the fruit of the Spirit, we arrive at the fifth characteristic Paul mentions: *kindness*. I will make another general comment about the fruit of the Spirit. We cannot help but see that they are beautiful. There is inherent beauty when we encounter a person or an act that is marked by love, joy, peace, patience, kindness, goodness, faithfulness, or self-control.

Their beauty is intensified in contrast to a world that is growing less and less beautiful every day. Don't misunderstand. I'm not a cynic who sees the world as completely spiraling into a state of evil and concludes that the world is going to hell in a handbasket. True, things are not as idyllic as I remember them in my childhood, but I take well the words recorded in Ecclesiastes 1:9: "What has been is what will be, and what has been done is what will be done; there is nothing new under the sun."

There certainly is great evil in the world today, but it is not new. There is also so much good. First of all, the narrative that the world is falling apart is driven in large part by fear. Second, the prevalence of communication technology and social media can put the hostility of this world on display in a way that it wasn't before. There is also a third reason we seem to believe the world is falling apart. The pain and suffering in the world is something of which we become increasingly aware as we get older, and we try to shield our children from it as well. As children, we see so much of the beauty and goodness in the world. As adults, we see the evil and suffering.

Kindness is something we emphasize with children and then think less about as adults. To prove my point: I am a little intimidated to talk about kindness in this book; and this is especially true when talking to a room full of elected leaders of state government. Kindness seems a bit trite—something we prioritize in children but something that becomes less important or relevant to address as we grow older.

It is unfortunate and tragic that our understanding of kindness should become so inverted because the antidote to pain and suffering—to all evil in the world—is kindness. Let me draw your attention to three realities about the nature of kindness. It is simple, universal, and a test of true religion.

Kindness is simple: there is nothing complicated about kindness, and it doesn't require a PhD to know whether or not you are being kind. Christian Nestell Bovee said, "Kindness is the language which the deaf can hear and the blind can see."[10]

Perhaps this is why we don't think too much of kindness when considering solutions to big problems or broken systems. Kindness is too simple. It lacks the sophistication or complexity that *important* things have. May I never be so arrogant as to believe that something simple cannot be profound. I hope I am never so blind that I cannot see how something simple can also have enormous power. King Solomon writes, "Kindness and truth preserve the king; And his throne is upholden by kindness."[11] This ancient and wise king believed it was kindness that kept the power and integrity of his authority intact.

It is true. There is something simple but undeniably beautiful when being kind. Among the great contributions of preeminent Catholic theologian Thomas Aquinas are his thoughts, found in his *Summa Theologica,* on what is known in the Latin as the *Transendentalia,* the Transcendentals.[12]

These are three transcendent qualities: the true, the good, and the beautiful. The idea is that there are things that are simply true. Others are simply good. Still others are simply beautiful. Not all things that are good are also beautiful, and not all things which are true are also good. But always pay attention when you come across something in this world that is at the same time true, good, and beautiful. When you find something like that, it may just be divine. In a simple act of kindness, we find something that is fundamentally true, absolutely good, and undeniably beautiful. What could be more profound? What simple act of kindness can you perform today?

Kindness is universal: I just mentioned the work of Aquinas, but the theological enterprise was never restricted to a particular faith or philosophy. People of various faiths across history have engaged in this work of thinking about the existence of God, the nature of God, whether or not God is reachable, and, if so, how one approaches Him:

> Confucius said, "Perfect virtue is the practice of five things under all circumstances: gravity, generosity of the soul, earnestness, sincerity, and kindness."[13]

The Dalai Lama said, "My religion is simple, there is no need for temples or complicated philosophy. My heart is my temple, my philosophy is kindness."[14]

Lao Tzu said, "Kindness in word creates confidence. Kindness in thinking creates profoundness. Kindness in giving creates love."[15]

The Greek Hellenists wrote, "No act of kindness, no matter how small, is ever wasted."[16]

Why do I share these quotes? Because I can show kindness to anyone, no matter who they are or whether or not they think or believe as I do. They can do the same for me. The virtue of kindness is both found in and appreciated by people of all walks of life.

Kindness is a test of true religion: James, the half-brother of Jesus who was later known as the great bishop of Jerusalem, writes, "Religion that is pure and undefiled before God the Father is this: to visit orphans and widows in their affliction, and to keep oneself unstained from the world."[17]

It is a two-pronged test. The first prong is this: as you grow older and gain greater awareness of the evil and suffering in the world, you should learn that there is a danger of being drawn into the evil of the world, to participate in and even perpetuate the corruption. James says to resist this.

There is a second prong to the test of true religion: to visit the widow and the orphan in their affliction. Widows and orphans were among the most marginalized of people in the first century. They were routinely denied justice, and society didn't see anything wrong with that. They had very little hope of ever rising out of their affliction.

In 2015, I led a mission team to Eastern Europe, and we stopped over in Greece in a town near the ancient city of Thessalonica. We were there to visit a Syrian refugee camp, and we drove up to a sea of white United Nations High Commissioner for Refugees (UNHCR) tents, where thousands of men, women, and children were living, having fled the horrors of civil war. We entered the camp and saw their living conditions. I talked with various people living in those conditions. As we entered the camp, we were quickly rushed by dozens of children, some as young as four years old. These children were orphaned. They left their homes with their parents and were either separated along the way, or, in many cases, their parents died.

These children had no parents, no passport, no country, no hope of leaving that camp, and most had witnessed unspeakable violence that I cannot begin to grasp. On that day, the face of the Syrian refugee crisis became the face of one six-year-old little girl. It is a face I will never forget.

Some of us returned home and began to engage in the situation in various capacities, following the prophet Micah's command to do justice, love mercy, and walk humbly with your God.[18] There are injustices that we can see, and the people of God are commanded, commissioned, and empowered to confront them. However, there are times when we face an injustice, a pain, or suffering that is just beyond us. I cried that night and pleaded with God because I needed to understand. We were overwhelmed in that camp. What could we do for them? I mean, what could we *really* do for them? There was nothing I could give, not even a bottle of water. Then I remembered this verse in James. "Religion that is pure and undefiled before God the Father is this: to visit orphans and widows in their affliction, and to keep oneself unstained from the world."[19] True religion was not taking the widow and orphan out of their affliction, resolving the affliction; rather, it was visiting them *in* their affliction.

So we smiled. We held their hands, and we played. Some started an epic game of fútbol, what we in America know as soccer. I had a deck of Mickey Mouse Club House numbered cards and began playing English and math games. These children knew their best chance to ever get out of that camp and have a better future was to learn math and English. I know that the Spirit of God was working through me because I am no English or math teacher. Yet, every time we came to the end of a game, somehow, I would come up with another, and we would play again. The joy and laughter from that six-year-old little girl echoes in my mind.

We didn't solve anyone's problems that day, and it is in God's hands that their story is not yet fully written. But I've never done or seen anything more important or profound than to confront very real pain with very simple kindness in that single moment.

Paul writes that the fruit of the Spirit is kindness because even when suffering is beyond you, kindness never is. God is near to the brokenhearted. God saves the crushed in spirit. He is going to them through you.

Why Do Good

Paul draws our attention to the next fruit of the Spirit, which is *goodness*. Like kindness, that which is *good* is far more significant than what may initially come to mind. I invite you to consider the nature of goodness through three questions: What is good? Is God good? And why do good?

What Is Good?

There are simple goods, things that are obviously beneficial or useful to our lives and world. There are personal goods, things that are good for an individual and not for anyone else. Then there are things that are good for many, maybe all people. There are those things which are good only for a moment and others that are good for generations. There are still other things that might potentially be eternally good. If greater good is possible, then is there something maximally good?

The seventeenth-century philosopher Gottfried Leibniz places the nature of goodness front and center when he asks whether or not there is a God. If there is, is God good? Leibniz concludes that God is good and characterizes God as *supremely good*.[20] If Leibniz is right and God is not just good but supremely good, what else is good?

The author of Genesis describes the nature of goodness by inviting the reader to observe the way in which God speaks all things into existence. Theologian John Walton explains the six-day creation account in the first chapter of Genesis by comparing it to the construction of a temple. The construction of a temple, as well as the subsequent cathedrals built throughout history, was an immense undertaking, a sacred task, and a generational endeavor.[21]

In the beginning, God creates the heavens and the earth. Walton presents these as two overlapping realities, one physical and one spiritual. God then adorns this temple in majesty, beauty, and wonder. He calls each act of creation good. A pastor I once served with was fond of saying, "At the words *let there be*, the darkness was pierced by a radiance never before known."[22]

Notice first, *the things God makes are good*: night and day, light and dark, sea and dry land. Walton suggests that God was creating for Himself a holy abode, a place in which He would dwell. Then God begins to fill this temple with plants and animals, the fish of the sea, birds of the air, and creatures upon the land. Each and every day of creation is a day of greater and compounding goodness, culminating in the pinnacle of creation: humanity.

Notice second, *humanity is good,* and by that I mean each human person is good. King David writes that God weaves each person together, body and soul. The author of Genesis writes that God then breathes into every person the very breath of life. The inherent good in each person transcends mind, body, and soul. It goes beyond what you do, think, feel, or say. It is not based on what you contribute or accomplish. You are good because you are alive, and this body that is fearfully and wonderfully made supports your life. Dallas Willard describes the significance of our physical bodies by thinking of the body as the instrument through which we communicate with God and with others. It is the means by which I can extend any good that is in me into the world around me.[23]

Notice now that *life is good.* The Bible begins with the tree of life placed in a garden, and it ends with that same tree of life placed in a city. The difference between the two is the population surrounding them. In the garden, there were two, and in that city, there is a multitude coming from every tribe and tongue and across all generations past, present, and future. With each generation, God brings more people into the world and into that city where with God they will one day dwell. Every day a child is born is a good day.

Even when life is not easy or in the midst of depression and despair, life is yet good. It is a tragedy when life is taken, either by the hand of another or by one's own. God alone is the author of life.

And last, in Genesis, we notice that *what God calls good, is good.* He did not simply see what He made was good. He deemed it to be good. In this way, God defines *goodness.* Nothing in the creation account was good inherently on its own but receives that quality and standard by virtue and decree of the One who made it.

Now for the moment of truth. All of this either holds together or falls apart on whether or not this God who creates and calls His creation good is Himself good. That is precisely how the Bible presents God. God is by His very nature good. God is the ultimate good. James writes that everything that is good actually comes down from the Father of Lights, from God. There is nothing good that didn't originate in God.

Is God Good?

But isn't that just what you would expect the Bible to say? We must honestly recognize there is problem or a conflict. At the very least, there is an apparent contradiction or dilemma that needs resolving. All around us, all of the time, we can see so much that is not good. We see people who are not good and who do not do what is good. I just said that every day a baby is born is a good day, yet Paul writes that we live in a present evil age and that the days are not good. Paul writes in Romans 7:18 that there is no good in me. Something's gone wrong or been corrupted. Even nature itself is extraordinarily cruel.

This begs the question of whether or not God really is good. With all that is not good, how can we trust that God is, in fact, good? We pray for healing and still succumb to disease. Parents suffer the loss of a child. There have been natural disasters and mass tragedies, and we know there will be more. Is God good?

In Luke 18:18, we read of the rich young ruler who comes to Jesus and asks, "Good teacher, what must I do to inherit eternal life?" This person of power, resources, influence, and authority recognized there was good in at least two things. First, the teachings of Jesus, and perhaps Jesus himself, were good. Second, eternal life was good. Jesus answers the rich young ruler and tells him what he needs to do to have eternal life. The rich young ruler's inclinations were right. Eternal life is good, and Jesus is going to tell him how to inherit it.

Before He does, Jesus asks in verse 19, "Why do you call me good? No one is good except God alone."[24] Responding this way, Jesus clearly teaches that God is good. In fact, God is the only One who is. There is no contradiction or conflict. What is more, God Himself has a plan to accomplish ultimate good because the offer of eternal life is still on the table, even for those who are not good or deserving. There is a remedy for all that has gone wrong and for all that is not good. It leads to an ultimate good. Do you believe Him?

This is the great test of faith. You may experience the very worst of what is evil and the apparent absence of hope. Especially when it is your own personal failure to do good that weighs the most, do you trust God is still good and intends good for you?

Can you say the following?

- Yes, even though I see so much bad in this world, there is good that confronts it.

- Yes, even if much of my life history, my childhood, my family, and my home is bad, my life is still destined for good.

- Yes, even if we are like lambs led to the slaughter, we are more than conquerors.

- Yes, what man meant for evil God meant for good.

- Yes, my Redeemer lives.

- Yes, God has the power to cause all things, even bad things, to work for my good.[25]

You can trust God is good when you understand that God is still in the business of creation. He is still speaking, but the words *let there be* now reverberate. *It is finished,* and the One who is seated on the throne says, "Look, I am making everything new."[26] What God makes He again calls good.

There was a remedy to all that is not good, but it required great sacrifice and came at a high cost. Is God good? He is good because God Himself paid it. When your faith is tested, what cause or reason do you have to trust God is good? Our faith is not a *blind hope in a distant creator.* It is beholding a *broken man on a debtor's cross.*

Now I can exclaim with the prophets, with Isaiah and Nahum, and with the Apostle Paul who declare how beautiful are the feet of those who bring good news.[27]

- Look at Jesus on the cross and see God is not ignorant or unconcerned about the pain and suffering in the world.

- Look at Jesus on the cross and see every evil deed in the past, present, and future has already and will one day be finally and fully reckoned and made right.

- Look at Jesus on the cross and see God recreating goodness in broken lives and hurting families by healing their wounds. God is reconciling, redeeming, and forgiving.

- Look at Jesus on the cross and see God, who did supremely good for you.

Paul writes the fruit of the Spirit is *goodness* because when you look at Jesus on the cross, you see the one who is good, did the greatest good, and, through His Spirit, now resides in you for good.

Why Do Good?

Let's turn our attention to a final question: why do good? It is an appropriate question to ask because, as much as I love the Bible, these are not intended as Bible studies but devotional messages that might encourage you, buoy your spirit, and inspire and motivate you. Most important, these were written with leaders in mind and in the hope that these nine virtues would be the qualities we desire to see more of in leaders.

As the title of this book implies, leaders matter. This is as true of elected leaders holding political office as it is of leaders in business and industry, churches, and local communities. We need them to lead our communities, companies, states, and nation to be good and to do good. Leaders serving in elected office know as well as anybody that the nature of goodness can be complicated. What is good for one person may not be good for another, and we live in a world of competing interests. However, all debate or disagreement evaporate when we find ourselves confronted with something so obviously not good.

That is how the great virtues work. You become acutely aware of the nature of peace when you don't have it or the extent of patience when pressed to your limits and what is kind when you are confronted with something cruel. So, why do good?

Reason 1: Do Good to Confront What Is Not Good

Like many, my stomach turned when reading the graffitied text and images of racist and anti-Semitic slurs defacing the entrances to public buildings, including an elementary school, across central Oklahoma in the spring of 2019.[28] Regardless of the specifics or motives, my heart sank to be reminded of an historic ideology principally aimed to rob a person of their humanity.

Such ideas are not new. History is replete with examples of people and whole nations that acted this way. But history is also filled with those who stood against such evil and confronted it with good.

The first response to why we should do good is clear: do good so that you might confront what is not good. Jesus told His followers to be salt and light in the world. He meant for them to live in contrast to all that is not good. His disciples are supposed to illuminate the good and expose the darkness.

The Apostle Peter taught that the best way to confront the bad and evil in the world is by doing good. He writes in 1 Peter 2:15, "For it is God's will that you silence the ignorance of foolish people by doing good." God will finally and fully respond to the bad. But, God's first response to the bad in the world is through our everyday acts of goodness that serve, love, and encourage those around us.

Reason 2: Do Good Because It Is Hard

Paul writes in Galatians 6:9, "Let us not grow weary of doing good." Why would he write that? Probably because doing good can be exhausting and cause us to grow weary!

Doing good is tiring because you are doing real things. In 2 Corinthians 5:10, Paul writes that God will judge everything we do in life, whether good or bad. The word for *bad* in Greek (*phaulos*) doesn't mean evil; it means worthless. In other words, when you do good things, you are doing things that matter, that have weight, that have value, that are worthwhile.

Doing good can be exhausting because, as I said before, we don't always agree on what is good—or what is best. Well, Paul has a solution. In Philippians 2:1-5, he pleads with his reader to set aside all selfish ambition and vain conceit, looking first to the good of others.

Thomas Aquinas defined love as *willing the good of the other*. Regardless of what it means for you, anything you do to promote the good of someone else, no matter how great or small, is a good thing.

But it will be tiring. Be encouraged. God knows. In Revelation 14:13, we read a conversation of sorts. A voice calls out and says, "Write this: Blessed are the dead who die in the Lord," and the Spirit of God responds, saying, "Blessed indeed, that they may rest from their labors." A life of doing good is a life of labor—but it is a life of love, marked by redemption and great reward.

The Spirit of God says, "Yes, may they rest from their labor," but goes on to say, "for their deeds follow them." When you do good, it has a ripple effect in the world and across time, bearing fruit and rewards that follow you into eternity.

Reason 3: Doing Good Was God's Plan for Humanity

Let's return to theologian John Walton. He compared the creation account in the first chapters of Genesis to the construction of a temple. When building a temple, the last thing that was added was the *icon*, often in the form of a statue. In Walton's view, the icon served two principle functions. The icon, first, identified the god or the deity for whom the temple was built, and, second, it directed worship toward that deity. In a sense, it drew the observer's attention in so that they could know what god was associated with that temple. With that understanding in place, the observer was then able to direct worship to that god.

God's creative work in Genesis 1 culminates in the pinnacle of His creation: humanity. Then, the author of Genesis says that God did something unique. He made humanity in the very image of God. If we keep with Walton's metaphor, humanity was uniquely made as the image bearers of the one, true Creator God. Humanity is placed in this great temple and serves that dual function. As living icons, every human person is designed to reflect God's image out into the world and direct all worship, adoration, and praise up to the God who made all things.

That was God's design for humanity, to reflect His very nature and His goodness into the world. Keep reading Genesis, and you quickly see the divine image became fractured and broken. To bear the image of God is nothing near being God. Reaching out to take the fruit and grasp it was to become like God. This is what the serpent told Eve would happen when eating the fruit from the tree of the knowledge of good and evil. It is prideful arrogance to believe that bearing God's image means one can also be God.

Believing I can take God's place is terrible folly and does violence to the very image of God within me. Yet, that belief is in the heart of us all and is the deep taproot of idolatry that underlies every selfish and evil act in history. When discussing the difficulty with keeping or breaking any of the Ten Commandments, the Protestant Reformer Martin Luther, writes, "The fundamental problem in law-breaking is always idolatry. In other words, we never break the other commandments without first breaking the commandment against idolatry."[29] The devastating consequences continue to wreak havoc in every generation.

With this view of creation, humanity, and history, I better understand the nature of evil. Where humanity was intended to reflect the image of a good and loving God, it was marred to instead reflect bigotry and racism, hatred and violence. People were intended to seek the good of others but instead act selfishly and cruelly. Everything I see in the world that is not good comes down to the abused and broken image of God that marks every person who ever lived and is yet to be born.

Despite the damage and in the face of all evidence that the divine image is broken, God's intended plan for us hasn't changed. The rest of the Bible tells the story of how God is getting us back to that place where we were in the garden. It's a story of redemption, healing, and a perfect restoration of the divine image of God back into humanity.

Romans 8:28 says that we know God is working in all things for the good of those who love God, who are called according to His purpose. The very next verse goes on to say that God has destined those very same to be conformed to the image of His Son. The divine image is being refashioned and remade in humanity.

Reason 4: Doing Good Is God's Unique Plan for You

His plan has not changed, and it is now His unique plan for you. Ephesians 2:10 says that we are God's masterpiece, created in His Son *for* good works that God Himself prepared ahead of time for us to do. They don't have to be big. They can be a simple act of kindness, a small gesture of love, just being a blessing to someone you meet in the hall or on your way home. There are good things for you to do today that were in the very mind of God since the foundations of the earth were laid. Don't ever believe what God has for you to do today is not significant.

You may be familiar with the story of the minister and hymn writer John Newton, best known for the song *Amazing Grace*. He was a sea captain, first in the royal navy and then as the captain of slave ships engaged in the transatlantic slave trade—another act of cruelty that robbed people of their humanity.

Over time, Newton became convicted of the heinous nature of his work, which led him to faith and ministry. One very simple act that was altogether good was to counsel a young William Wilberforce, a member of parliament who was struggling with his own call to remain in parliament or serve God in ministry. Newton essentially told him to do both, and Wilberforce became a most ardent and effective legislator leading to the abolition of the slave trade in Britain. Wilberforce's story inspired thousands to follow his example, and countless good has resulted across time since.[30]

Reason 5: Do Good Because You Still Have Time

Throughout their history of affliction, the nation of Israel sang a familiar refrain that is repeated across the psalms: *How long, oh, Lord?* This is my great solace when evil rears its head. Ultimately, I ask God to deal justly with the evil in the world because that responsibility is beyond me. The Scriptures consistently call God good while promising He will not leave the guilty unpunished: "The LORD is slow to anger but great in power; the LORD will never leave the guilty unpunished."[31]

Ecclesiastes 12:14 promises that God will bring every deed into judgement, including every thought, whether good or bad. God is not blind to the evil in the world, and there is a day coming where every wrong will be made right.

The question isn't *whether or not God will deal justly with the evil*, but *why has He not yet done it*? That question is not new. Again, the ancient psalmists cry out: "LORD, how long will the wicked – how long will the wicked celebrate?"[32] God alone knows the answer, but it is partly because there is still good for us to do, and there is still time to do it.

Paul writes that the fruit of the Spirit is *goodness*, knowing that a day of perfect justice is coming. Until that day comes, whenever such darkness shows up in the world, may it remind us that we have another day to confront it with good—a chance to be another John Newton, William Wilberforce, or Apostle Paul.

Chapter 12

Who Lead with Faithfulness, Gentleness, and Self-Control

Way of Faithfulness

With *faithfulness*, we are nearing the end of the Paul's list of the fruit of the Spirit. What does it mean to be faithful? How do you define *faith*? It is a central question to the human condition.

Historically speaking, recognizing the importance of faith was crystalized in the founding of America. This is clearly evident in the development of the concept of *soul-freedom*, the liberty for every person to hold a particular faith and practice that faith freely. Soul-freedom is among the great contributions to the American experience that can be traced back to Roger Williams, John Leland, and James Madison. The first two held soul-freedom as a central faith distinctive. Williams was instrumental in the founding of the Rhode Island Colony. Leland pressed leaders such as James Madison for the importance of a Bill of Rights that enshrines religious liberty in the establishment clause of the First Amendment, protecting the religious freedom of all Americans.

From a biblical perspective, faithfulness is consistently tied to God's love for us and to salvation:

- "Let your faithful love come to me, Lord, your salvation, as you promised."[1]
- "Give thanks to the LORD, for he is good; his faithful love endures forever."[2]
- "God's faithful love is constant."[3]

Faithfulness is also tied to a personal experience through a relationship between a person and God.

- "In keeping with your faithful love, hear my voice. LORD, give me life in keeping with your justice."[4]
- "May your faithful love comfort me as you promised your servant."[5]

It could help to think of being unfaithful in terms of relationship. In human relationships, particularly in marriage, the concept of infidelity is quickly understood. But infidelity in marriage doesn't have to be solely connected to physical unfaithfulness. Trust can be broken in a number of ways. Faithfulness is a long-standing love, an unfailing commitment to always make the good of *this* particular person your priority.

That understanding of faithfulness rings true with the picture painted in Scripture. There are other words and phrases used in Scripture that are just another way of describing faith, such as *belief*, *trust*, or the *fear of the Lord*:

- "The fear of the Lord is the beginning of knowledge."[6]
- "Trust in the LORD with all your heart, and do not rely on your own understanding; in all your ways know him, and he will make your paths straight."[7]

So how do you define *faith*? One prevailing way culture defines faith can be stated as *holding a belief in the absence of apparent evidence or reason*. A leap of faith, so to speak. I am highly critical of this understanding of faith, and I trust I'm in good company. For centuries, theologians argued the unique capacity to reason, to think critically and freely is what the Bible means when it says we are created in the image of God.

Let's seek a better understanding of faith. The psalms and the prophets repeatedly exhort the reader to trust in God's promised word, which gives comfort, hope, and life.[8] I encourage you to consider faith as meaningful direction for your life, the path to Truth that has integrity and internal consistency, and life-giving strength when trials come.

Faith Gives Meaningful Direction for Your Life

When encountering difficult decisions or considering courses of action to take, opportunities to pursue, or potential relationships, faith may very well be the best, and sometimes only, resource to call upon. When you boil away specifics and circumstances, faith gives an answer to existential questions: Where are you headed? What is guiding you?

When we read the gospels, Jesus is always calling people to a new way, a new path, and a new purpose. The earliest Christian churches were actually referred to as followers of "the way." Some were religious leaders. Others were fishermen. Some of Jesus' followers were tax collectors and even government officials. It is the same in our day; Christians come from a wide array of backgrounds, vocations, ethnicities, nationalities, religious traditions, and walks of life. Unbelievably, in the midst of such diversity in the Christian faith—every person's way is totally unique and circumstances are vast and varied—every person's way begins the exactly the same. Jesus says, "Come, follow me."

How do you follow Jesus? Let's speak plainly and make every effort to avoid churchy language or Christian jargon. There are many ways *not* to follow Jesus, and one best way you can.

Don't follow Jesus at a distance. It may be true when following Jesus at a distance that you will still go in the right general direction, but you'll make missteps along the way. Those missteps can cause pain in your life and in the life of others. They can also make you think your decisions, abilities, and actions are better than they really are.

Don't run out in front of Jesus. Resist the temptation to run out in front of Jesus as you experience the zeal and excitement that comes when you *think* you see where He is leading you. When you find yourself out in front of Jesus, you can't see Him. You lose your bearings, and you're left to yourself to choose which way to go. Going the way you want to go works great—until it doesn't. When things stop working so well, you are left to your own devices to respond. This presents another opportunity for missteps and complications.

Don't try to walk side-by-side with Jesus. By this, I'm imagining myself as linking arms with Jesus and walking down a path together as friends. It sounds good. Unfortunately, you will inevitably try to pull Him in the direction *you want to go*, and that is wrestling. You will not win.

The best way to follow Jesus is by staying just one step behind Him. Put your foot down where His was just set. It can be difficult. Most of us want to see what is at the end of the path or where Jesus is leading. This method rarely shows that to you. But it is how the Christian faith gives meaningful direction to your life. Every step. Every day.

Faith Is a Path to Truth with Integrity and Internal Consistency

There are many philosophies and religious traditions that, by and large, are offering a path to knowing truth. Perhaps the most pressing of all the conflicts in the Western world today is the collision of these diverse philosophies and opposing worldviews. What makes this conflict so important is not the collision itself but the need for a path to truth that has both integrity and internal consistency.

One book that was a game changer in my understanding of the integrity and internal consistency of the Christian faith was J.P. Moreland's *Love God with All Your Mind*. The title of his book is taken from a famous passage found in the Gospel of Matthew where Jesus says, "Love the Lord your God with all your heart, with all your soul, and with all your mind."[9]

In his book, Moreland writes, "For many, religion is identified with subjective feelings, sincere motives, personal piety, and blind faith."[10] The results have been disastrous. Moreland goes on to write, "God is certainly not a cultural elitist, and He does not love intellectuals more than anyone else. But it needs to be said in the same breath that ignorance is not a Christian virtue."[11] It was already stated that faith is not an abandonment of reason. Enduring faith demands we do the hard work and employ critical thinking. In the words of the twentieth-century Christian apologist and author C.S. Lewis, "[Christ] wants a child's heart, but a grown-up's mind."[12]

Ultimately, faith is a system of belief. The question is, does yours hold water? For the answer to that question to truly be yes, that system of belief cannot be relative to time or culture. You have a serious problem if the faith you hold will work in the suburbs of middle America but falls apart on the streets of Tehran or in a prison cell in Asia. Psalm 119:90 says, "Your faithfulness is for all generations; you established the earth and it stands firm." The gospel found in the Christian faith transcends time, culture, generations, and borders. It is hope for the middle school student in south Saint Louis and for the Coptic Christian facing martyrdom in Northern Egypt.

We could spend a lifetime on this one point, and far better minds than mine have. What I challenge you to do is this: ask the hard questions of your faith and see if there is integrity and internal consistency. When the answers are not forthcoming, it is faith that stays the course. God is not offended or afraid of hard questions. When writing to people who were facing all sorts of difficulty and persecution, the author of James writes, "Now if any of you lacks wisdom, he should ask God—who gives to all generously and ungrudgingly—and it will be given to him."[13]

However, James goes on to say, "But let him ask in faith without doubting. For the doubter is like the surging sea, driven and tossed by the wind. That person should not expect to receive anything from the Lord, being double-minded and unstable in all his ways."[14] A double-minded person is someone who asks God for wisdom but reserves the right not to follow it. A faithful person asks God for wisdom, already trusting it is God's best and is for their greatest good. A faithful person trusts that is true, even if it is not what you want to hear. Enduring faith can lead us to hard truths, but these truths have integrity.

Faith Is Life-Giving Strength When Trials Come

Finally, when the questions do persist or when the difficulties are great, faith gives life that thrives anyway. Faith that is life-sustaining is vital, particularly when things get hard or when you're not getting to where you thought you were going or wanted to go. It isn't much comfort to discover the Bible teaches that God tests our faith. Have you ever wondered why God tests our faith? The reason our faith is tested, British author and pastor David Pawson teaches, is because God is not interested in a pet; He is developing a child, an heir, a friend.

At the end of John's Gospel, we read of Jesus talking to Peter and restoring him. This is after Peter rejected even knowing Jesus on the night Jesus was betrayed. Peter is told his path will be one of greatness but also of great suffering. Peter cannot help but look at John and say, "Lord, what about him?" Jesus tells Peter not to worry about John. What Jesus intends for John is irrelevant to Peter. If I put myself in Peter's place, what I am essentially hearing Jesus say is this: if you are going to do what I'm calling *you* to do—the hardest thing you'll ever do—you have to keep your eyes on Me.

Understand faith this way: not as a blind leap but as a bold trust that gives direction to your life. Faith is a path to truth that has integrity. Faith is life-giving strength that is sustaining. With this understanding of faith, Paul can write that the fruit of the Spirit is faithfulness because it is from the Spirit of the One who called Himself the Way, the Truth, and the Life. If your faith is in Jesus, then keep your eyes on Him and stay just one step behind.

Gentleness Is the Fruit Applied

Each year, spring fever seems to grip me by the throat. Warmer weather and evenings around a fire pit are what I live for at that time of year—and baseball is back!

One of my very good friends in high school was a phenomenal player and got picked up right after our senior year by a major league ball club. Within three years, he was a starting left-handed pitcher for Pittsburgh.

Each year, in the off season, my buddy would come back home for a few weeks, and we'd all hang out as much as possible. One night, we were all out to dinner and ended up playing pool. I'm not a great pool player now, but back then? Well, we were all better at things like that in college, weren't we? I was playing pool against my friend, the major league pitcher, and I ran the table on him— twice, as I remember it.

I couldn't help myself, and the trash talk just flowed out of me with each shot made. He just sat there, with a calm smile on his face. After I was finally done, he quietly stood up and looked at me. He picked up the eight ball and said, "Joel, I never said I was any good at pool, but grab that cue, stand over there, and let me throw this at you." His point was made.

I know it's not a perfect illustration. We weren't exactly playing his game, so to speak. The point is that my friend knew very well the truth about his strength and ability, as well as my lack of both. Rather than unleashing all his strength, precision, and skill on me, he offered a gentle word that taught me a lesson I have not forgotten. He was much more than he seemed in that moment.

The next to last virtue on Paul's list of the fruit of the Spirit is *gentleness*. It is a characteristic that we don't often talk about, possibly because gentleness can look to others as nothing more than weakness. When we do talk about gentleness, the words and ideas we prefer might be compassion or humility. Another word for *gentleness* that somehow seems more palatable is one that is often interchangeable in the Bible: *meekness*.

We do this because we want to be very clear that we are not talking about being weak. Weakness is a real thing. An important part of parenting is helping your child discover their own strength and then navigate fears and obstacles so they will not fall prey to them. We don't like weakness. Quite the opposite is true. We like strength. One of my favorite definitions of *meekness* is a common one that is probably familiar: strength under control. That is exactly what my friend, the major league pitcher, was that night.

There are a lot of similarities between the idea of gentleness and the idea of self-control. It would be easier to talk about self-control. But, self-control is the final virtue Paul includes in his list and one we must consider separately.

Gentleness deserves full attention, and it is unfortunate how we can give it so little. The nineteenth-century Dutch pastor George Bethune once said, "Perhaps no grace is less prayed for, less cultivated than gentleness. Indeed, it is considered as belonging to external manners, rather than as a Christian virtue; and seldom do we reflect that not to be gentle is sin."[15] That is certainly one reason to pay a little more attention to gentleness.

Another is remembering that this exploration of the nine virtues listed in the fruit of the Spirit is set in the context of the things we need in leaders. When considering leaders, and as a leader, consider three reasons why you should aspire to be gentle.

1. Gentleness Is the Best Indication That Wisdom Is Governing Your Heart and Mind

Being governed by wisdom is a vital need of political leaders and policy makers, especially when they dialogue and debate. This is true with a friend and is especially true when it is with someone of an opposing view.

Writing to Timothy, who was a leader in the church in Ephesus at the time, Paul said, "The Lord's servant must not quarrel, but must be gentle to everyone, able to teach, and patient, instructing his opponents with gentleness."[16] James was the leader of the church in Jerusalem, when he wrote this about wisdom: "Who among you is wise and understanding? By his good conduct he should show that his works are done in the gentleness that comes from wisdom."[17]

Leadership will require you to stand up for what is right and against what is not. But a wise leader challenges a position or perspective that they believe to be in error without making an enemy of their opponent.

"A gentle answer turns away anger, but a harsh word stirs up wrath."[18] We should avoid angry and ultimately useless quarreling. Rather, we need leaders who give us fruitful debate.

To paraphrase President Harry Truman, leadership is getting a group of people to do something they don't want to do in order to gain a better future. With this definition, a leader must question the reasons why people don't want to do whatever it is they believe is needed. Perhaps the reason is not because what they are currently doing is bad or wrong but because they haven't considered the future they are being led to. Accomplishing that is hard work. But it would be an impossible task, and people would never consider that potential future if they don't trust their leader or their leader's motives. Wisdom marked by gentleness breeds trust.

What James writes next is vital to leaders: "But if you have bitter envy and selfish ambition in your heart, don't boast and deny the truth."[19] As a leader, if you have any selfish ambition or bitter jealousy, James is saying that your leadership is only deception. You are deceiving those you desire to lead. More than that, you deceive yourself and are not the leader you think yourself to be.

2. Gentleness Is God's Own Model of Effective and Needed Leadership

When the prophet Isaiah, was writing about God's leadership, he said, "[God] protects his flock like a shepherd; he gathers the lambs in his arms and carries them in the fold of his garment. He gently leads those that are nursing."[20]

Whatever you think of Jesus as a prophet, teacher, or messiah, consider how He describes Himself as a leader to His disciples: "Come to me, all of you who are weary and burdened, and I will give you rest. Take my yoke and learn from me, because I am lowly and gentle in spirit, and you will find rest for your souls."[21]

They got it. Peter, who could hardly be called weak, described true beauty as, "What is inside the heart—the imperishable quality of a gentle and quiet spirit, which of great worth in God's sight."[22]

3. Gentleness Is the Evidence of All Other Virtues at Work, Transforming Your Heart and Life

If you want to know whether or not there is an increase of love, joy, peace, patience, kindness, or goodness in your life, then ask yourself this question: do I see any evidence of gentleness in me?

After Paul writes this full list of the fruit of the Spirit, he offers a practical application. It is a scenario where the reader is meant to put them into practice. In Galatians 6:1, Paul writes, "If someone is overtaken in any transgression, you who are spiritual, restore them with a gentle spirit."

He doesn't say a loving spirit or a joyous or patient or peaceful spirit. Paul says, do it with all of them, and it will look like gentleness. Let's analyze this hypothetical scenario. The phrase "overtaken in any transgression" can also be translated as "caught, trapped, or fallen."

The word picture that Paul is painting is of someone who is running a race, a familiar metaphor he uses. This person who is running the race loses their footing and falls. They don't just stumble; they fall completely flat on their face. They are prone and lying on the ground. Full stop. Perhaps it was an unseen obstacle, an injustice, or a tragedy beyond their control that caused them to fall. Most often, the fall is of their own doing by mistakes or missteps. They tripped themselves. Nevertheless, there they lie.

Paul says that those of you who are spiritual—and in this sense, we can think of those who have the fruit of the Spirit operating in their lives—are to restore them. But they are to restore them in one specific way: gently. You don't just hitch your arm under theirs and let your momentum pull them up. Neither do you jog in place and bark at them. Telling them they shouldn't have done what they did or, worse, stating the obvious isn't effective: "Hey, you're on the ground!" Those methods of restoring are sadly pretty common among people who think themselves spiritual.

Restoring someone gently means stopping where they are and sitting down on the ground next to them. Full stop. Tend to their pain. Help them to a seated position, then a kneeling one, and then help them up on their feet, letting them lean on you. Then walk beside them until you start gaining momentum and are both running again. Paul says, be careful not to fall yourself. He means don't take your eyes off the better future that awaits them and you. Do this until you are both running at full pace again. But gentleness helps them to get there one step at a time.

Paul writes the fruit of the Spirit is gentleness because it is the very evidence of all the others. Without gentleness, you can never lead those who most need your strength, wisdom, vision, and help.

Full Freedom in Self-Control

Jesus' life, teaching, and work was marked by power and authority. It was said He taught as One who had authority. He was a miracle worker. Many people left their homes and jobs to follow Him as His disciples.

After His triumphal entry into Jerusalem, the Pharisees questioned Jesus in Matt. 21:23, asking, "By what authority are you doing these things? Who gave you this authority?" His authority was a threat to their own, and they were looking for a way to undermine and destabilize His authority. If they could do that, they would further establish their own. Jesus responds by asking them a question: "Did John's baptism come from heaven, or was it of human origin?"[23] He made a deal with His Pharisee inquisitors. If they answered His question, then He would answer theirs.

It was a clever question, and they were stumped. John baptized Jesus, and if they responded that John's baptism was from heaven, from God, then how could they deny it? If from human origin, it would affirm the people's authority. The Pharisees were aware of the crowds who welcomed Jesus into Jerusalem and their cries of "Hosanna" and "Blessed is the King who comes in the name of the Lord."[24] The Pharisees feared the power of the people and knew that many who followed John believed him to be a true prophet. To validate their authority would be to acknowledge their belief in Jesus as the King in the line of David. In the end, the Pharisees refused to answer.

But the Pharisees asked a good question: where did Jesus' authority come from? Even today, any who study the life of Jesus should ask this question. But I would also ask, where does any of our power or authority come from? Once having it, what is the best way to approach authority and use it?

Paul closes his list of the fruit of the Spirit with a virtue that is, in itself, the indication of ultimate power, authority, and strength: *self-control*. In my study of the Bible, I find this principle to be constant: the truest measure of strength is not by comparing my strength to another's or by competing with them but by bringing my strength under the subjection of my own will. Consider this simple principle of physics. There is no power, ability, sheer determination, or might that is greater than the power, ability, determination, or might required to subdue it.

As strong as you ever believe yourself to be is weaker than the strength within yourself to be self-controlled. How powerful are you? This is not a benign question. We need strong leaders.

Writing his second letter to Timothy, Paul encourages his friend and protégé in the role he has as leader of a church. But Paul also recognized a tendency in Timothy toward timidity. We don't know the exact reason for Timothy's diffidence. Whatever the reason isn't important because Paul knew that we don't need timid leaders. We need strong ones. Paul reminds Timothy that God has not given us a spirit of fear, but one of power—and not just of power but also of love and self-control.[25]

The spirit of power, love, and self-control is the ability to respond in love when the circumstances are pressing us to respond with hate or when the world tells us we can do whatever we want or think is right. This is especially true of those who are in authority and possess power and strength; theirs should be an ability to be self-controlled and use sound judgment.

Paul knew effective leadership begins with people who are self-controlled. That is as true today as it was in Paul's day. We should ask of our leaders that they be people who are self-controlled. Leaders can learn self-control by asking the same question the Pharisees did: *where does Jesus' authority come from*? Consider three possible answers to that question. Jesus' authority either came from God, from Himself, or from the people who followed Him.

1. Did Jesus' Authority Come from God?

The significance, impact, and influence of the life of Jesus Christ is a fact of history that is undisputed by modern scholars. Whatever I may think, it is equally undisputed that Jesus believed His authority came from God. Having received authority from God, Jesus responded by humbling Himself under that higher source of authority.

Jesus said, "Truly I tell you, the Son is not able to do anything on his own, but only what he sees the Father doing," and, "for I have not spoken on my own, but the Father himself who sent me has given me a command to say everything I have said."[26] Through humility and self-control, Jesus boldly acted and spoke with *all* the authority He believed God gave Him—no more and no less.

Leaders should take note of this. By this example of Jesus, we learn that when authority comes from something above us, we can boldly exercise every ounce of that power. But it is self-control that keeps us from abusing authority. Self-control keeps us from taking even one step beyond it. We need leaders who will boldly exercise authority—no more but no less.

2. Did Jesus' Authority Come from Himself?

The leaders of the early church believed Jesus was God. The author of Genesis taught it was through the power of the word of God that everything was created. With this understanding, John called Jesus the very same Word of God in His Gospel account. In Colossians, Paul called Jesus the "image of the invisible God."[27] What did Jesus believe about his own identity? C.S. Lewis asked that question. Lewis concluded that Jesus believed He was God and famously noted that Jesus was either a liar, lunatic, or Lord.[28]

One of the greatest and most poetic passages in the New Testament, which tells us what the early Christians believed about the identity of Jesus, is found in Philippians 2:6-11. Paul is imploring the people to humble themselves and to look first to the needs of others. Paul then says the Christians were to have the mind of Christ, whom He gives as the ultimate example of self-control and humility.

In that passage in Philippians, Paul describes Jesus as being in His very nature God, but He did not consider equality with God as something to grasp. The image of Jesus grasping for equality with God is striking. It invokes the memory of Adam and Eve in the garden. They are told by the serpent to take the fruit that God said they should not take. The serpent said, take the fruit, and you will be like God. All they had to do was reach out and grasp it.

In contrast, Jesus holds equality with God in His hand from the beginning but lets it go. That act of self-control is described as Jesus *emptying Himself*, and it is probably the most mysterious phrase in the whole New Testament: *kenosis*, the act of Jesus emptying Himself. What sort of strength is required to harness the power of God in your hand and let go of it? That act gives Jesus the right to tell me I should deny myself: "Then he said to them all, 'If anyone wants to follow after me, let him deny himself, take up his cross daily, and follow me.'"[29]

Our tendency is to think the pinnacle of God's attributes might be holiness or omnipotence. I suggest that the highest of God's attributes is really humility. Humility is the very mind of Christ. It is why both Peter and James say, if you want to become exalted and reach the height of human potential, then humble yourself before God.[30]

In Philippians 2:6-11, reaching the height of human potential is exactly how the poem ends. Because Jesus humbled Himself to the point of ultimate humiliation, God exalted Him to the highest place. Self-control is what kept Jesus from imposing His nature and authority onto people. Anything else would undo all that Jesus believed He was sent to do. Leaders should take note and learn by this example. Jesus knew that over-confidence in your own ability, skill, strength, or power inevitably leads to arrogance.

Arrogance and overconfidence destroys leaders and compromises the good they do. Paul writes to the Corinthian church that leaders should work hard to remain self-controlled. He offers himself as an example and concludes that without self-control, he might become disqualified even after being an effective leader.[31]

History is filled with leaders who disqualified themselves. They trusted so much in their own ability and power that they became prideful and arrogant, ultimately forfeiting their authority.

3. Did Jesus' Authority Come from the People Who Followed Him?

I once had a conversation with a member of the Oklahoma House of Representatives who asked me what I thought was the greatest temptation Jesus ever faced. We talked about it and then this honorable representative told me they believed it was when the devil showed Jesus all the kingdoms of the world. It's possible this included every nation across all of human history and all the people within them. We can find this in Matthew's Gospel: "Again, the devil took him to a very high mountain and showed him all the kingdoms of the world and their splendor. And he said to him, 'I will give you all these things if you will fall down and worship me.'"[32]

Essentially, the devil says, "I will give You their splendor and all this authority. If You will just worship me, then it's Yours." Stated another way, "I'll let everyone know who You really are, and then they will *have* to serve You."

But that is the catch. The people will *have* to serve Him. It was self-control that allowed Jesus to resist and remember that if any authority from the people was to have significance, then it must be freely given. This is the great contrast between Jesus and the Pharisees, such as the ones who questioned Him. It is why He would not answer them.

The Pharisees subjected people to restrictions and limitations. They imposed their interpretation of the law and righteousness onto the people. When it came to their interpretation of the law, the Pharisees were not guilty of being illiterate. They knew what the law said, but they missed the spirit of those words. The law was meant to connect people to God.

The Pharisees derived their authority by forcing people into subjection. Jesus derived His authority by setting people free: free from their own faults and failures and free from all of society's divisions. The freedom from Jesus invites all people to come together because all are welcome at Jesus' table, where all people can connect to God. And freedom from Jesus transcends culture, creed, generation, and nation.

Remember from the very first discussion in this section, *The Last of Human Freedoms*, that the fruit of the Spirit is a discussion of what a heart that has been set free looks like. No matter what is happening around you or what is happening inside you, there can be an inner fortitude of the soul. There is power and authority that cannot be taken away, no matter what the external circumstances are. It is power to be free as we were intended.

Paul writes the fruit of the Spirit is self-control because it is the ability that harnesses the fullness of human freedom, power, and authority. Self-control is the path to the height of human potential through the humility of the son of God. When leaders cultivate self-control:

- They will exercise authority they possess without abusing it—no more but no less.

- They will bring the fullness of their skills, talent, and experience to bear but not fall victim to pride or arrogance and become disqualified.

- They will have the trust and respect of the people they represent and lead because the people will freely give it.

The Result

★ ★ ★ ★ ★

Producing Civility and Integrity

Not only must we be careful to want and desire good things . . .
but also to want and desire them in a way that is good.

—Father Jacques Philippe[1]

You can design and create, and build the most wonderful place
in the world. But it takes people to make the dream a reality.

—Walt Disney[2]

Chapter 13

In Current Leaders

Be a yardstick of quality. Some people aren't used to
an environment where excellence is expected.

—Steve Jobs[1]

The Paradox of Freedom

If you recall, the chapter in Galatians where Paul lists the fruit of the Spirit opens with the statement, "For freedom, Christ set us free."[2] The human heart was meant to be free, and we have considered each of these nine human virtues as Paul painting a robust picture of what human freedom looks like. Freedom is a deep liberty of soul that cannot be taken away, no matter the conditions or circumstances. It is comprised of the following:

- Love never ends and is the very language of heaven that we are only learning to speak.

- Joy is a longing for purpose, home, and friendship, regardless of situation or circumstance.

- Peace enables us to endure both chaos and conflict, but more important, we reflect the peace of God into that conflict.

- Patience gives us the strength to bear more than we ever could.

- Kindness is that which is fundamentally true, absolutely good, and undeniably beautiful.

- Goodness is the power to confront all that is evil in our world.

- Faithfulness is not a blind leap but a bold trust that gives direction, truth with integrity, and life that is sustaining.

- Gentleness is the evidence of all the other virtues and allows us to lead.

- Self-Control is the ability to harness the fullness of human freedom, power, and authority.

Now that the picture of freedom is in full view, we ask one last question: what do you do with it? Paul already told us: it is *for* freedom you have been set free. Freedom is for freedom's sake. The next few verses in Galatians chapter six clarify that Paul intends us to know that having been set free, we are now bound to the cause of freedom. This is the beautiful paradox of freedom.

Paul was one of the most ardent advocates for full freedom in God. His work and writing broke down traditional barriers of race, gender, socio-economic status, nationalism, imperialism, and religion. Yet, on multiple occasions, this great evangelist of freedom refers to himself as a bond-servant to Christ.[3] Paul knew that it was not a yoke of slavery but of salvation. He knew that Jesus told His disciples to take His yoke upon them and learn from Him, "for my yoke is easy and my burden is light."[4]

The paradox continues. Being set free for freedom's sake entails the following:

- It will take you to the point of exhaustion but will always bring you rest.

- It will make you question what you are to do at times but is a fixed point guiding your steps.

- It may challenge what you think is true while remaining the greatest truth you've ever known.

- It will demand everything of you but is not a burden.

The one thing freedom will not do is leave us alone to do nothing. A few verses later, Paul writes, "Don't be deceived: God is not mocked. For whatever a person sows he will also reap."[5] It is true that there are wicked, prideful, and selfish things we can sow in life. Make no mistake. Understand that we will reap pain, destruction, and brokenness in due time.

Laying that aside, Paul is teaching that we are either putting these virtues into practice or not. Let me be vulnerable for a moment. I can honestly look at this full list of nine virtues and know pretty quickly that I'm not firing on all cylinders. There are times that I may be doing well with six of them, or three, or maybe just one. But that is alright and precisely why we took the time to look at the virtues independently. Each one is beautiful, powerful, and desperately needed, especially from leaders.

Among the more significant things I came to believe since moving from Washington DC to Oklahoma, where I've been able to meet and know leaders of every kind, is that we desperately need state and local leaders who are governed by and inspiring others with peace, patience, love, joy, kindness, goodness, faithfulness, gentleness, and self-control.

There is opportunity for leadership marked by these nine qualities to set people free in every community across our state and nation. We need state and local officials to lead us with these virtues wherever they can. We also need leaders with the humility to recognize where they are lacking. In those areas, these leaders will lean on others around them who are strong.

Not any one of us has mastered them all. We all grow in the areas where we are weak. Most important, we invite others to lean on us in the areas where we are strong. This is how to live for freedom's sake. "Carry one another's burdens," is how Paul writes it, "in this way you will fulfill the law of Christ."[6]

What does it look like to carry one another's burdens?

- When there is someone you know or will encounter whose situation is cruel, for freedom's sake, your simple act of kindness shines bright in their darkness.

- When all the forces in our culture are pressing us to hate or to fear, for freedom's sake, you possess love that drives out fear.

- When someone is suffering pain or tragedy, for freedom's sake, confront it with goodness that soothes their sorrow.

- When we become discouraged by the division and strife that seems to have gripped our nation and world, for freedom's sake, project a deep peace of the soul into the conflict, quieting the noise and rebuilding trust and confidence in the integrity of our still great society.

Yes, it is for freedom's sake we have been set free. When you are not sure if it is really within you, remember that Paul calls them fruit of the *Spirit* because whatever you lack, the Spirit of God provides. Listen to these promises across history and throughout Scripture.

- "So do not fear, for I am with you; do not be dismayed, for I am your God. I will strengthen you and help you; I will uphold you with my righteous right hand."[7]

- "Those who seek the Lord lack no good thing."[8]

- "The Lord is near to all who call on him, to all who call on him in truth."[9]

- "My grace is sufficient for you, for my power is made perfect in weakness."[10]

- "He gives power to the weak and strength to the powerless."[11]

- "For God has not given us a spirit of fear, but one of power, love and of sound judgment."[12]

These nine virtues are common to all people and can be found in every corner of the earth. But Paul writes of them as the product that comes from knowing God because each of them point to the nature, character, person, and purpose of God. The fruit of the Spirit paint a picture of a fully free heart. They also depict the nature of a forever faithful God.

Paul draws his letter to the churches in Galatia to a close by writing, "Let us not get tired of doing good, for we will reap at the proper time if we don't give up. Therefore, as we have opportunity, let us work for the good of all."[13]

We are not unaware that doing good is hard work. Those stepping into a position of leadership, who hope to accomplish good things that will benefit all people, know well their work is exhausting. This scripture is a warning that working for the good of all people will be tiring, to the point one is tempted to give up.

Don't give up. Don't grow tired in doing good because we know that the hard work of putting these virtues into practice doesn't result in reaping the benefits today. They come at the proper time when they will result in the greatest good for all. We pray the work of leaders will result in greater freedom for everyone. Leaders have an immense opportunity to promote greater freedom because the work they do affects many. But the fruit of the Spirit is for all of us—not just for leaders. Working for the good of all is what this deep freedom of the soul is really meant for and that is what we can do.

Chapter 14

★ ★ ★ ★ ★

In Future Leaders

*I will not follow where the path may lead, but I will go
where there is no path, and I will leave a trail.*

—Muriel Strode[1]

Elements Required to Create Change

Changing culture requires three important elements. First, *we
need to know what we will accomplish.* This means understanding what
the problem is and truly believing the change we are making is the
right answer. The problem in our culture is the heightened incivility plaguing the political discourse, which leads to a society that is
increasingly divided and hostile to opposing points of view. Discov-
ering the ability to respect leaders, whether or not we agree with
them, will restore the civility we need *in our politics* and promote
the integrity and servant leadership we need *in our leaders.* When
that happens, they will be able to work and lead our communities,
states, and nation to address the real problems we are facing and
navigate a way forward that will bless and benefit all of us.

Second, *we need the courage to act.* One of the direct results of this
approach to engaging leaders is the rediscovery of your own authority and, with it, the ability to make your voice heard. It really does
start with you. As you join your voice with others asking better for

our political discourse, the incivility and vitriol dividing our culture will dissipate.

Third, *we need a strategy that will ensure success.* The strategy is to begin with leaders, starting with those closest to where you live and work. Start with state and local leaders and engage them with the three steps of believing leaders matter, asking more for leaders, and asking more of leaders. Let's quickly recap the process.

The first step is to *believe* leaders matter and understand how they serve a vital function in society. Leaders possess the authority to create solutions to our most pressing problems and inspire us to be better than we are. The first step also emphasizes the importance of remembering that leaders are *people*. When we remember that leaders are people just like you and me, we become more compassionate to the everyday struggles and challenges that we all have.

Step two is asking more *for* leaders by desiring the best for them as a person. While power and authority exist and are necessary components in the world, there is a difference between the positions of leadership where power is found and the individuals who are in those positions. The position is not the same as the person. Remember to ask more for leaders following three important principles: being thankful for them, desiring the best for them, and setting aside any other agenda as you do so. We should desire that our leaders are healthy and remember they have families and other responsibilities beyond their public trust. Just as you have hopes for your own life, desire your leaders' homes be safe and filled with joy.

Step three is to ask more *of* leaders. Now that you are able to better distinguish between the leadership position and the person in that place of authority, you can better approach them and interact with respect and sincerity. This garners real opportunities to ask more of leaders. Before you ask anything else of a leader, remember that what we need most in a leader is that they are a person of integrity. What if the leader has so compromised their integrity that they legitimately lose your respect? This is the most beautiful part of this approach.

When a leader clearly lacks integrity, you know *precisely what* to ask for them. Pray they become a person governed by love for others. Pray they become a person filled with joy, peace, and patience. Pray they become kinder and gentler in their lives and leadership so they can work better for the good of all people and discover self-control. These are nine marks of integrity we need in leaders, and there are others. This approach is not naïve or idealistic. This is a practical, effective, and powerful way to engage and influence leaders to be, work, and serve better.

Ways to Engage

Now is the time to engage leaders with these three steps, and here are a few ways to get started.

On social media: For good or for bad, politics is a game played on Twitter. Social media creates unprecedented access to elected leaders and is increasingly becoming an important way in which governmental entities communicate important information to us. Here is a simple rule to remember about interacting on social media: being negative accomplishes almost nothing, but being positive can accomplish almost anything. Never underestimate the power of 140 characters to encourage the very heart and soul of a person. Imagine what would happen in the state capitol if elected leaders were receiving hundreds of messages each day or week similar to this:

> "Hello, Representative, thank you for the work you are doing to serve our community/state today!"

> "Senator, I wanted you to know I prayed for you and your family today!"

"Representative, I prayed for you to have wisdom and joy as you work at the Capitol this week!"

Through their office: Leaders do not work alone. Elected leaders are surrounded by individuals assisting them in their task, and when choosing to engage, a good place to begin is with their staff. Call their office, send an email, or write a letter. In most cases, every piece of constituent communication is seen by someone on staff who has a process for addressing the constituent's questions and responding. Cultivating a meaningful relationship with a leader often begins by cultivating a relationship with their staff. As the front line of engagement with an elected leader, staff members bear the brunt of the anger and hostility directed at their boss. That also means they are the first person touched by the respect, encouragement, and sincere prayer for their boss. They are the gatekeepers who open the doors to meaningful connection with elected leaders, and they also address the real needs constituents have. More important, they need the encouragement, too.

In person (and in the community): One of the greatest opportunities you can have to engage an elected leader is when they are back home in their district. Find an event in your community where your representative or senator will be speaking and make a point to shake their hand. Being present is important as a chaplain, and nothing replaces looking someone in the eye when encouraging them. When elected leaders see the same person—who consistently demonstrates respect and gratitude—at a few events, they remember and may even begin seeking them out at future events. That is the sort of relationship we can build with leaders to make the greatest impact over the course of their political career.

Becoming the Leader We Need

We can recover civility, integrity, and servant leadership in American political discourse. We are all responsible for our culture, and each of us have a voice and the ability to shape a positive leadership culture that breaks through the incivility. But it will require more of us. We must get involved and champion the character and integrity we want. We can disagree without being disrespectful or abandoning our principles and convictions.

We will not always agree, but we can create a culture of respect and goodwill that allows leaders to skillfully navigate those disagreements and solve real problems. You have the ability to help the people in positions of authority so they can promote the civility, integrity, and the leadership we need right now. If you are the sort of person who will engage those who are currently in positions of authority *believing* leaders matter, asking more *for* them, and asking more *of* them, then chances are, you are the sort of person who will one day be the kind of leader we need. You likely already are.

Notes

Introduction: Ask More *of* Leaders by Asking More *for* Leaders

1   R. E. Olson, *The Mosaic Of Christian Belief: Twenty Centuries of Unity and Diversity*, (Downers Grove, IL: InterVarsity Press, 2002), 90.

2   Ibid., 89, 95.

3   John Wesley, *Explanatory Notes upon the New Testament*, (London: Epworth Press, 1948), 794.

4   Prov. 9:10, emphasis added.

5   D. G. Bloesch, *Holy Scripture: Revelation, Inspiration & Interpretation*, (Downers Grove: InterVarsity Press, 1994), 129.

6   Olson, 106.

7   S. B. Ferguson, D. F. Wright, & J. I. Packer, *New Dictionary of Theology*, (Downers Grove: InterVarsity Press, 1988), 627.

8   See Eph. 1:3-14.

9   Olson, 106.

10   See Acts 20:27, 30, 32.

11   2 Tim. 3:16-17.

12   See Rom. 12:1-2.

13   M. J. Wilkins, *Following the Master: Discipleship in the Steps of Jesus*, (Grand Rapids: Zondervan, 1992), 42.

14   Rom. 8:28-29.

15   Phi. 1:6.

16   John Stott, "Four Ways Christians Can Influence the World," *Christianity Today*, Oct. 20, 2011, https://www.christianitytoday.com/ct/2011/october/saltlight.html.

17   Mike Metzger, *Fine Tuning Tensions within Culture: The Art of Being Salt and Light* (Suwannee, GA: Relevate, 2007), 4.

Step One: *Believe* Leaders Matter

1   Tricia McDermott, "Ronald Reagan Remembered," *60 Minutes*, 2004, https://www.cbsnews.com/news/ronald-reagan-remembered/.

2   President Jimmy Carter, June 21, 2016, https://www.cartercenter.org/news/editorials_speeches/a-time-for-peace-06212016.html.

Chapter 1: When Shaping the Leadership Culture

1   Paulo Coelho, Interview with United Nations News Center, 2015, https://paulocoelhoblog.com/2015/03/13/intercultural-dialogue/.

[2] A. C. Brooks, *Love Your Enemies: How Decent People Can Save America from Our Culture of Contempt*, (New York: HarperCollins, 2019), 4.

[3] Ibid., 5.

[4] Ibid., 214.

[5] Aristotle, *Politics*, 5.8.8.

[6] D. Erasmus, L. Jardine, N. M. Cheshire, & M. J. Heath, *The Education of a Christian Prince*, (Cambridge: Cambridge University Press, 1997), 69.

[7] Civility in America, 2019, https://www.webershandwick.com/wp-content/uploads/2019/06/CivilityInAmerica2019SolutionsforTomorrow.pdf.

[8] C. Porath & C. Pearson, "The Price of Incivility." *Harvard Business Review*, Jan-Feb 2013.

[9] Ibid.

[10] Ibid.

[11] Ex. 22:28.

[12] J. O. Buswell, *A Systematic Theology of the Christian Religion*, (Grand Rapids: Zondervan, 1984), 403-404.

[13] Matt. 22:21.

[14] David Pawson, *Unlocking the Bible: A Unique Overview of the Whole Bible*, (Travelers Rest: True Potential Publishing, 2007), 577.

[15] See Jer. 29:1:1-2.

[16] See Dan. 1-6.

[17] See Ex. 20:3-5.

[18] Dan. 3:18.

[19] See Dan. 3:18.

[20] Martin Luther King Jr.'s *Letter from a Birmingham Jail*, from R. A. Goldwin & M. L. King, *Civil Disobedience: Five Essays by Martin Luther King, Jr. [and others]*, (Gambier, OH: Public Affairs Conference Center, Kenyon College, 1968).

[21] Dan. 3:17-18.

[22] Charles Colson, 1996, BreakPoint: *Dunkirk, "And if Not"* https://www.christianheadlines.com/columnists/breakpoint/dunkirk-and-if-not-the-story-behind-the-story.html.

[23] Dan. 6:21-22.

[24] Zaid Jilani, "The Hidden Benefits of Disagreeing about Politics," *Greater Good Magazine*, September 13, 2019, https://greatergood.berkeley.edu/article/item/the_hidden_benefit_of_disagreeing_about_politics.

[25] Tim Keller, *Counterfeit Gods: The Empty Promises of Money, Sex, and Power, and the Only Hope That Matters*, (New York: Dutton, 2009), 99.

[26] President Jimmy Carter, June 21, 2016, https://www.cartercenter.org/news/editorials_speeches/a-time-for-peace-06212016.html.

NOTES
★ ★ ★ ★ ★

[27] From interview with *PBS NewsHour*, July 31, 2018, https://www.pbs.org/newshour/show/the-problem-with-fear-in-politics.

[28] See Josh. 1:9.

[29] See Rom. 8:15, Galatians 4:6.

[30] See 1 John 4:18.

[31] See 1 Cor. 13.

[32] See 1 John 4:8.

Chapter 2: When Making Your Voice Heard

[1] S. A. McChrystal, J. Eggers, & J. Mangone, *Leaders: Myth and Reality*, (New York: Penguin Random House, 2018), 241.

[2] Titus 3:1-2.

[3] B. R. Ashford & H. Thomas, *The Gospel of Our King: Bible, Worldview, and the Mission of Every Christian*, (Grand Rapids: Baker Academic, 2019), 170.

[4] Michael Shinagel, Harvard University, 2019, https://www.extension.harvard.edu/professional-development/instructor/michael-shinagel.

[5] R. A. Mohler, *The Conviction to Lead: 25 Principles for Leadership That Matters*, (Minneapolis: Bethany House, 2012), 99.

[6] McChrystal et al., 20.

[7] Ibid., 10.

[8] Ibid., 7.

[9] Ibid., 8.

[10] Ibid., 9.

[11] Mohler, 19.

[12] R. A. Heifetz, *Leadership without Easy Answers*, (Cambridge, MS: Harvard University Press, 1994), 235.

[13] John 19:10-11, emphasis added.

[14] Heifetz, 49.

[15] Ibid., 65.

[16] Ibid.,104-105.

[17] Ibid., 49.

[18] Ibid., 73.

Chapter 3: When We Need a Strategy

[1] Joan Magretta, *Understanding Michael Porter: The Essential Guide to Competition and Strategy*, (Boston: Harvard Business Press, 2010), 140.

[2] Stephen Hawkins, et al., "Hidden Tribes: A Study of America's Polarized Landscape," *More in Common*, 2018, https://hiddentribes.us/pdf/hidden_tribes_report.pdf.

[3] Brooks, 26-27.

4   Ibid., 29.
5   See Rom. 1:16.
6   W. Barclay, *The Letters to the Philippians, Colossians, and Thessalonians*, rev.
    ed. (Philadelphia: Westminster Press, 1975), 3.
7   See Matt. 5:44.
8   Es. 4:13-14.
9   See Jer. 29:7 (ESV).
10 Prov. 29:2.

Chapter 4: When We Need a Different Perspective
1   Sen-ts'an, *Hsin hsin ming*. In Conze 1954.
2   1 Tim. 2:1-4.
3   1 Tim. 1:18 (ESV).
4   William Shakespeare, *Henry V*, Act IV, Scene iii.
5   1 Tim. 1:19.
6   See Eccles. 12:14.
7   See Phil.1:27.
8   1 Tim. 1:12-14.
9   1 Tim. 1:15 (ESV).
10 Interview with *Face the Nation*, May 28, 2017.
11 Ps. 46:6.
12 See Matt. 28:18-20.
13 See Rom. 13:1, 4.
14 W. W. Wiersbe, *Be Mature: An Expository Study of the Epistle of James*,
    (Wheaton: Victor Books, 1978), 118.
15 From Heifetz.
16 See James 3:9-10 (ESV).
17 From Heifetz, 263-264.
18 James 5:16 (ESV).

Step Two: Ask More *for* Leaders
1   D. E. Hiebert, "The Significance of Christian Intercession," Bibliotheca
    Sacra 140:558 (January-March 1992), 16-26.
2   J. Stott, "Four Way Christians Can Influence the World," Christianity
    Today, October 20, 2011, christianitytoday.com/ct/2011/october/saltlight.
    html

Chapter 5: Through Prayer
1   O. Chambers, My Utmost for His Highest, (Grand Rapids: Discovery
    House Publishers, 2005), 17.

NOTES
★ ★ ★ ★ ★

[2] See 1 Tim. 2:1-4.

[3] Rom.13:4.

[4] Comments invented by the author for illustrative purposes. Not actual quotes.

[5] 1 Tim. 2:2.

[6] Brooks, 58.

[7] Ibid., 40.

[8] Ibid., 41.

[9] Ibid.

[10] See Matt. 28:18-20.

[11] See Matt. 16:18.

Chapter 6: Because We All Can Pray

[1] Hiebert

[2] Pawson, 577.

[3] See Ps. 19:13.

[4] James 5:13-14.

[5] James 5:15.

[6] James 5:16.

[7] See 1 John 1:9.

[8] See Matt. 6:10.

[9] A.W. Tozer, *The Pursuit of God*, (Colorado Springs: Christian Publications, 1963), 83.

Chapter 7: Invocations from a Capitol Chaplain

[1] See Ex. 20:8-11.

[2] See Ps. 37:1-8, author paraphrase.

[3] See Ps. 33:13-15.

[4] See Ps. 33:16, 18-22.

[5] See Ps. 46:1-2.

[6] Psalm 46:10, author paraphrase.

[7] See Ps. 24:1.

[8] See Eccles. 7:14.

[9] See Eccles. 7:8-9, emphasis added.

[10] See Ps. 119:89-93.

[11] See Ps. 25:4-7.

[12] See Ps. 119:49-50.

[13] See Isa. 55:9.

[14] See Isa. 12:1-3.

[15] See Ps. 67:1.

16 See Ps. 66:5, 7, 20.
17 See Joel 2:1, 12
18 See Prov. 16:1-3.
19 See Prov. 16:4.
20 See Ps. 12:7.
21 See Ps. 47:7-9.
22 Gal. 5:1
23 See Ps. 144:2

Chapter 8: Taming the Tongue
1   See James 1:2-3.
2   Paraphrase from Barclay, 144-145.
3   See James 1:4.
4   See James 2:1-13.
5   See James 1:27.
6   See James 5:1-6.
7   See James 4:4-5.
8   See James. 2:15.
9   See James 3:2.
10 See James 3:8.
11 See James 3:5.
12 See Job 9:19-20.
13 See James 3:9.
14 See James 3:11-12.

Step Three: Ask More *of* Leaders
1   *ForbesQuotes*, 2019, https://www.forbes.com/quotes/2301/.

Chapter 9: Who Lead with Integrity
1   J. R. Clinton, *The Making of a Leader: Recognizing the Lessons and Stages of Leadership Development*, rev. ed. (Colorado Springs: NavPress, 2012).
2   Ibid., 51.
3   Ibid., 50.
4   Galatians 5:1
5   A. Redsand & V. E. Frankl, *Viktor Frankl: A Life Worth Living,* (New York: Clarion Books, 2006).
6   V. E. Frankl, *Man's Search For Meaning: An Introduction to Logotherapy,* 3rd ed. (New York: Simon & Schuster, 1984), 86.

NOTES
★ ★ ★ ★ ★

Chapter 10: Who Lead with Love, Joy, and Peace

[1] Thomas Aquinas, *Summa Theologica*, I-II, Question 26, Article 4. This is often translated as "To love is to will the good of another."

[2] See 1 Cori. 13:4, 7.

[3] See Rom. 8:35-37.

[4] Paul L Maier, ed. *Eusebius: The Church History: A New Translation with Commentary*, (Grand Rapids: Kregel, 1999), 112.

[5] D. A. Carson, 2000, *Crossway Books*.

[6] See James 1:17, emphasis added.

[7] D. Bonhoeffer, *The Cost of Discipleship*, (New York: Touchstone, 2012), 34.

[8] Victor Hugo, *Les Miserables*, trans. Charles E. Wilbour, (New York: Random House, 1992), 506.

[9] Anxiety and Depression Association of America, https://adaa.org/about-adaa/press-room/facts-statistics.

[10] C. S. Lewis, *Surprised By Joy: The Shape of My Early Life*, (London: G. Bles, 1955).

[11] See Luke 22:42.

[12] See Nehemiah 8:10

[13] Philippians 3:10

[14] C. H. Spurgeon, *The Treasury of David*, vol. 1, (Peabody: Hendrickson Publishers, 1990), 339.

[15] John Ronald Reuel Tolkien, *The Hobbit, or, There and Back Again.* (New York: Ballantine Books, 1982).

[16] See Ps. 46:4 (ESV).

[17] See Luke 2:10.

[18] W. G. Lambert & S. B. Parker, *Enuma Elis: The Babylonian Epic of Creation*, (Oxford: Clarendon P, 1966).

[19] See Gen. 1.

[20] See Isa. 9:6.

[21] Ps. 24:3.

[22] Matt. 19:25-26.

[23] Charles Haddon Spurgeon, *Spurgeon's Sermons*, vol. 7, 1861, Lulu.com, 312.

[24] Ibid., 313.

[25] See Phil. 4:7.

[26] See John 14:1.

[27] J. Philippe, *Searching for and Maintaining Peace: A Small Treatise on Peace of Heart*, (New York: Alba House, 2002), 5.

Chapter 11: Who Lead with Patience, Kindness, and Goodness

[1] See Jo. 4:2.

2   2 Pet. 3:9 (NIV).

3   See Matt. 18:21-22 (NIV).

4   William Barclay, *New Testament Words*, (Westminster: John Knox Press, 1964), 145.

5   James 1:4.

6   See Phil. 1:6.

7   See Phil. 2:16; Gal. 2:2; Gal. 5:7; 2 Tim. 4:7

8   See Heb. 12:1

9   See Heb. 12:1-2.

10 C. N. Bovee, *Thoughts, Feelings, and Fancies*, (New York: Wiley and Halstead, 1857), 109.

11 See Prov. 20:28 (ASV).

12 Aquinas.

13 Confucius & N. B. W. Van, *Confucius and the Analects: New Essays*, (Oxford: Oxford University Press, 2002).

14 Joseph Demakis. *The Ultimate Book of Quotations*, (Scotts Valley: CreateSpace Independent Publishing Platform, 2012), 333.

15 Andy Zubko. *Treasury of Spiritual Wisdom: A Collection of 10,000 Powerful Quotations for Transforming Your Life*, (Delhi: Motilal Banarsidass, 2000), 283.

16 Aesop, *Aesop's Fables: No Act of Kindness, No Matter How Small, Is Ever Wasted*, (Scotts Valley: CreateSpace Independent Publishing Platform, 2018).

17 James 1:27 (ESV).

18 Mic. 6:8.

19 Jas. 1:27 (ESV).

20 G. W. Leibniz & N. Jolley, *The Cambridge Companion to Leibniz*, (Cambridge: Cambridge University Press, 1995), 404.

21 John Walton, *The Lost World of Genesis One* (Downers Grove: InterVarsity Press, 2009).

22 Rev. F. Don Davidson, First Baptist Church of Alexandria, VA (2005-present).

23 D. Willard, *The Spirit of the Disciplines: Understanding How God Changes Lives*, 1st ed. (San Francisco: Harper & Row, 1988), 52-55.

24 See Luke 18:19.

25 See Rom. 8:28.

26 See Rev. 21:5.

27 See Isa. 52:7; Nah. 1:15

NOTES
★ ★ ★ ★ ★

[28] Joel Harder, "Point of View: Responding to Vandalism, Racism, and Hate," *The Oklahoman*, 2019, https://oklahoman.com/article/5627896/point-of-view-three-ways-to-respond-to-hate-vandalism.

[29] Martin Luther, *A Treatise on Good Works*, part X, XI.

[30] Eric Metaxes, *Amazing Grace: And the Heroic Campaign to End Slavery*, (San Francisco: HarperOne, 2007).

[31] Nah. 1:3.

[32] Ps. 94:3.

Chapter 12: Who Lead with Faithfulness, Gentleness, and Self-Control

[1] See Ps. 119:41.

[2] See Ps. 118:1.

[3] See Ps. 52:1.

[4] See Ps. 119:149.

[5] See Ps. 119:76.

[6] See Prov. 1:7.

[7] See Prov. 3:5-6.

[8] See Ps. 119:49-50.

[9] See Matt. 22:37.

[10] J. P. Moreland & D. Willard, *Love Your God with All Your Mind: The Role of Reason in the Life of the Soul*, (Colorado Springs: NavPress, 1997), 26.

[11] Ibid., 45.

[12] C. S. Lewis, *Mere Christianity: A Revised and Amplified Edition, with a New Introduction, of the Three Books; Broadcast Talks; Christian Behaviour; Beyond Personality*, (San Francisco: HarperSanFrancisco, 2001), 77.

[13] See James 1:5.

[14] See James 1:6-8.

[15] George W. Bethune, *The Fruit of the Spirit*, (Swengel, PA: Reiner, 1893), 100.

[16] 2 Tim. 2:24-25.

[17] James 3:13.

[18] Prov. 15:1.

[19] James 3:14.

[20] Isa. 40:11.

[21] Matt. 11:28-29.

[22] 1 Pet. 3:4.

[23] Matt. 21:25.

[24] See Mark 11:9; Luke 19:38.

[25] See 2 Tim. 1:7.

[26] See John 5:19; 12:49.

[27] See Col. 1:15.

[28] Lewis, *Mere Christianity*, 55.

[29] Luke 9:23.

[30] See 1 Pet. 5:6, James 4:10.

[31] See 1 Cor. 9:27.

[32] See Matt. 4:8-9.

The Result: Producing Civility and Integrity

[1] J. Philippe, *Searching For and Maintaining Peace: A Small Treatise on Peace of Heart*, (New York: Alba House, 2002), 52.

[2] S. A. McChrystal, J. Eggers, & J. Mangone, *Leaders: Myth and Reality*, (New York: Penguin Random House, 2018), 49.

Chapter 13: In Current Leaders

[1] F. Filloux, "Steve Jobs: Seven Lessons from Apple's Founder," *The Guardian*, 2011, https://www.theguardian.com/technology/blog/2011/oct/10/steve-jobs-seven-lessons.

[2] Gal. 5:1

[3] See Rom. 1:1; Gal. 1:10; Col. 4:7; 2 Tim. 2:24; Tit. 1:1

[4] Matt. 11:30

[5] See Gal. 6:7.

[6] Gal. 6:2.

[7] See Isa. 41:10 (NIV).

[8] See Ps. 34:10 (NIV).

[9] See Ps. 145:18 (NIV).

[10] See 2 Cor. 12:9 (NIV).

[11] See Isa. 40:29 (NLT).

[12] See 2 Tim.1:7.

[13] See Gal. 6:9-10.

Chapter 14: In Future Leaders

[1] Muriel Strode, "Wind-Wafted Flowers," *The Open Court* 1903, no. 8(5), https://opensiuc.lib.siu.edu/ocj/vol1903/iss8/5.

Author Contact

If you would like to contact Dr. Harder, find out more information, purchase books, or request him to speak, please contact him at:

www.JoelWHarder.com

Follow Dr. Harder!
https://twitter.com/JoelWHarder
https://www.facebook.com/DrJoelWHarder